THE TRIALS OF FREDDY GOODCHILD

FREDDY KING ESQ

COPYRIGHTS

Copyright ©2025 *Freddy King Esq*

All rights reserved.

TABLE OF CONTENTS

Chapter 1 1
Chapter 2 8
Chapter 3 13
Chapter 4 18
Chapter 5 23
Chapter 6 28
Chapter 7 91
Chapter 8 97
Chapter 9 104
Chapter 10 110
Chapter 11 117
Chapter 12 120
Chapter 13 130
Chapter 14 136
Chapter 15 147
Chapter 16 151
Chapter 17 156
Chapter 18 161
Chapter 19 167
Chapter 20 170
Chapter 21 174
Chapter 22 182

Chapter 23 189
Chapter 24 194
Chapter 25 206
Chapter 26 214
Chapter 27 217
Chapter 28 227
Chapter 29 235

CHAPTER 1

Freddy Goodchild was born in the north eastern industrial town of Middlesbrough, in the middle of the Second World War. He was an only child. His world was Park Lane and the surrounding streets and near a park opened and championed by Prince Albert husband of Queen Victoria. The houses were built in the nineteenth century for workers in the local industries. At his young age everything seemed vast including the park which had areas where places appeared mysterious. From his bedroom window he could see over the high wall opposite his house into the maternity hospital. The gardens were beautifully kept by the resident gardener and beyond he could see the trees and open spaces of Albert Park. He spent many happy hours playing with the local boys on the hill called Bell's Hill in the park, probably named after the bell that had been placed at the top of the hill.

He was quite small for his age but he was very popular with the local children. His home was nearly always deserted as his family members were frequently absent, which is why he spent so much time away from his house. In those times it was not unusual for children to be left alone as very few came to mishap. The house was an old, rented, Victorian, corner, town house built during the early establishment of the industrial environment in the North East of England. The Steel Works were a major employer in Middlesbrough. The property was a 'two up, two down' building but with a totally abandoned second floor that at some time had been a bathroom and a bedroom that was under the sloping roof of the house but was now in a sad state of repair. The upper house had been abandoned for some time and was just bare dusty boards on the floor and no furniture of any sort.

At the junction outside of the house was a large re-enforced concrete community bomb shelter and in the front garden was an Anderson bomb shelter. As well as the bomb shelters the house and back yard were excellent places to play without interruption or observation from adult intervention. His father was never known by him and the mother never lived down the shame of an unmarried pregnancy but the shame was purely in his mother's mind. Many of the local girls had been left alone with a child for a variety of reasons. War time was like that.

Without a father and a mother who would not speak of any father or any mentor from family or friends, he grew up self-reliant and street wise. The home was only a place to sleep or play when empty and his education was acquired from his peer group and the related groups of down town urchins. The war left the town scarred through the frequent attempts by the German air force to bomb the steel and chemical works that provided the main employment and income for the town. The industry provided a massive contribution to the British war effort. All the metal garden gates and railings had been smelted down for arms and bullets at the local iron and steel works. The bomb damage to the local area was a perfect playground for the youngsters. Even the town centre had been heavily bombed and many of the main stores were just open cellars after the rubble had been cleared.

The air raid shelters were used as dens and the bombed houses were great for hide and seek. Freddy Goodchild, as a very young child, spent his days in the local nursery where many of his happier memories were located. His mother earned a meagre living as a 'Clippy' on the buses. The varied shifts of the work pattern meant that his mother was very rarely at home for significant periods of time. When she was at home the number of 'uncles' that visited the house were beyond the understanding of young Freddy but the gifts that he received from uncles, given to 'go and play', were very welcome and Freddy was only too pleased to oblige. One 'uncle Freddy' gave him a heavy overcoat and in the pocket was a half crown. In those days half a crown was a fortune. On that occasion he was, of course, told to leave the house and go and show all of his friends his new coat. He was surprised at the number of family members that came to visit and he was surprised at the large family to which he appeared to be a part. Strangely he never saw the associated Aunties.

His time at nursery school was a joy for him. Nurse Pallister was one of the nursery staff and she became a substitute mother figure for him. The nursery was located at the end of Park Lane through the only gate in the high wall that stretched the length of the lane. It was a very private and beautifully appointed nursey for children from all backgrounds but restricted to only twenty in number. Those were his memorable happy days of that time of his life. In later years he frequently visited the elderly Nurse Pallister who was always very interested in Freddy's activities and progress.

Freddy left the nursery school and moved on to the local primary school at Victoria Road. and his education on the subject of girls blossomed. The school was built by the Victorians and it was a solid old building with a playground within high brick walls. The upper school was privileged with a steel posted fence that gave a view through the bars to Victoria Road and the outside world. The school rooms had windows well above the height of any occupant in the building, ensuring that there was no distraction by the outside world. Celia was just one of the attractive girls who seemed fascinated by the difference between the sexes and Freddy learned that his genitals were not just for physical comfort. Celia seemed to get great pleasure from handling Freddy's parts under the desk whilst the teacher attempted to impart knowledge at the blackboard. This activity did, in fact, cause some distraction from the teaching. Billy went to school with Freddy and they frequently met at Billy's house. The house was about fifty yards and around the corner from Freddy's house in Granville Road.

His parents like Freddy's were always working until late at one of the local hostelries. They worked at the Westminster Pub on Parliament Road and Billy had the run of the house just about every evening. His older brothers had girl friends around on a regular basis, all in party mood and Celia was a guest of Freddy's on many occasions. That was the time that Freddy realized what was happening at his house after hearing and seeing the upstairs activities and the knowledge made him feel even more isolated.

When his mother married, it was to a very new 'uncle' called Peter who was a bus driver at the bus depot where she worked. Peter was a dour soul and he had a very limited sense of humour, I suppose that one could call him a typical simple Yorkshireman, simple being the operative word. Peter was from a quite large family with relations all over the County of Yorkshire. His uncle Jack was the head reader at the Yorkshire Post newspaper. Jack lived directly opposite the Headingly cricket ground and matches could be seen and followed from the upstairs front room. In his teenage years many a happy time was spent there watching Yorkshire cricketers take on the best teams in the country.

The wedding was paid for by the groom's parents and they insisted on a church wedding. It was all very grand but Freddy was not invited. He was an embarrassment for his mother as she was being wed in white. This fact was vehemently referred to by Freddy's grandmother to all persons that she encountered. It was only years later that Freddy found out that his grandmother had never been married. The wedding was obviously not a love match as the number of visiting uncles did not diminish and there was obvious resentment from Peter towards another man's child in his marriage. Arguments frequently occurred at home and Freddys' parents did not talk to each other for weeks on end. They communicated through terse notes left for each other to find. The atmosphere at home was quite toxic for a lot of the time. Freddy became the ball to be kicked to and fro during the frantic discussions.

    Freddy spent most of his time outside of the home playing in bomb damaged buildings and the Anderson and Communal air raid shelters that still remained after the war. They were usually in poor condition, with a foot of water in the bases of the Anderson shelters and varied refuse left after the many activities that occurred in the Communal shelters. Life changed radically when they left his grandfather's rented house in Park Lane and moved into a brand-new house on a council estate at Beechwood.

    The house was on the south side of the estate and facing open countryside. The fields, trees and streams were a revelation to Freddy. He had never seen greenery outside of the local park which, to him, was real countryside, as it was surrounded by railings, even though it was sternly patrolled by a very grumpy and intolerant Park Keeper. The window from his bedroom gave views, not of high walls and fences but of distant hills and farm lands, cows, sheep and horses. The horses astounded him. He had seen the local coal man on his cart delivering his loads of coal but the horses from his window were sleek, powerful animals which were totally different from the heavy, tired, lumbering beasts of burden that he was used to seeing. The Lamp Lighter no longer came round the roads riding his bicycle with his long pole to turn on the gas and light the gas filament with the flame at the end of his pole. The electric lights came on as if by magic. It was a wild and massive new playground which afforded every opportunity to spend lots of time away from the house and the discord atmosphere in there.

Now only the most persistent one or two uncles came and went. Just over a year later, Freddy passed the scholarship, the eleven plus and elected to go to the only real grammar school in the area. The only response that he got from home was 'how did you manage that?' Acklam Hall Grammar School was three miles away from the estate across open fields and streams, some occupied by cows and sometimes bulls. Freddy learned not to dawdle when crossing fields and his ability and speed for running developed. The bull population was very fast for their size. The headmaster had very little time for council estate students and took every opportunity to embarrass or punish any child with that background. Freddy took his revenge on the headmaster in his final year when the decorators arrived to cover the work of the student toilet artists and school wits. The head appeared to be a funny purple colour as he climbed on stage at the final morning assembly.

The whole School was totally aware of recent happenings and were trying very hard not to explode into laughter as the head spluttered out his disapproval and vague threats against the perpetrators. He had arrived at his prestigious and historic school to find 'Joe's Cafe' painted, in six- foot-high capital letters, on the roof. It could be seen for miles, glowing in the twilight and glaring in the day's sunlight advertising the school to all far and wide. The black knickers and brassieres hoisted up to the top of the flag pole did nothing to sweeten his mood on the last day of term. The underwear had been kindly donated by girls from the adjacent all-girls school. Some of the governors were ex-students and found the whole incident hilarious. The final day was Presentation Day and the Governors took the stage for the awards. After the awards it was the custom to congratulate the school and its' students on the year's achievements but the Chair of Governors could not resist a mildly supportive comment towards the culprits. They had a sneaky feeling of admiration wishing that they had thought of it when they were students. Freddy left the school with a respectable number of 'O' and 'A' levels at GCE. Freddy's parents were too busy with their own lives to even comment on his final report.

CHAPTER 2

His mother's brother, Derek, had joined the Royal Air Force some years before and always promoted an exciting image with photographs of himself with his buddies during the Suez crisis. One story came from a picture sent from Egypt of Derek and his buddies in the desert near the Suez Canal with a detail on the picture of a round black mark on Derek's chest. His note was to confirm it was a print error and not a bullet hole. Freddy was truly impressed with the photographs and took the opportunity on leaving school and after a variety of casual employments, he joined up and became an airman. He wanted to be a pilot and applied for aircrew. The basic aircrew training was undertaken by all applicants and selection for aircrew posts was a one-day aptitude assessment.

Things did not go well for the selection. Freddy was delayed by administrative duties. He told the duty officer about the selection times but the officer was Administration Staff and resented the 'Brylcream Boys' and their rapid promotion, so he was as awkward as possible. The selection and the pilot familiarisation had finished before he arrived. He was thrown straight into the test, totally unprepared. He did, however, finish top in the navigation selection and was sent to Navigation training school. During his training period Freddy spent his leave periods at home but mostly visiting Nurse Pallister. She was always interested in his progress through his life. Having qualified he was sent on his first posting and after extensive operational experience the story begins.

Freddy was posted and allocated to the flight crew that included 'Pinky' James. The only commissioned officer on board was a Flying Officer Radio Operator who was more inexperienced than any other crew member. He had led a very sheltered life and was completely out of place and treated as a junior member of the crew. He did, however, own an MG sports car which was very useful for evening excursions for the crew. Pinky James was the highly respected crew leader as he was a decorated and very experienced master pilot. He had distinguished himself during the second world war with a large number of confirmed kills.

Although Pinky was a great deal older Freddy and he hit it off straight away and developed a friendship that took them visiting many of the district watering holes in the MG. Flying Officer Peebles was a welcome chauffeur. The story begins when they were transferred to lead an operation which was as the supply squadron to overseas forces posted to Germany and it became a once a week, one day return, flight. The type of aircraft was a great disappointment to Pinky but the fact that it was a weekly trip abroad cheered him. The chance to partake of cheaper 'grog' made Pinky very sensitive to the Varsity aircraft faults on landing and therefore had all checks made to the aircraft before returning to base. The Varsity plane was known as the 'Flying Pig', and from its' appearance and handling it was easy to see why. The number of faults, strangely occurring, always, of course, meant an overnight stay and a night in the sergeants' mess bar.

It became a routine and on one such occasion they arrived in the mess bar. "You threw the kite down today, Pinky, is there a problem?" "I needed to do something to wake you up." said Pinky. "It's a wonder you Navigators find the right country never mind the right ruddy airfield." "And God bless you too." said Freddy. "You are welcome," said Pinky "I am getting bored out of my skull with this milk run, it always seems to pour with rain whenever we land in Germany, why can't we get something more exciting, it's not as if the crew lack experience and there are lots of things going on all over the world, a little bit of active service would help."

As they sat in the following silence two very attractive ladies came into the mess. Freddy had seen them before and he had wondered how they gained entry to the Mess unaccompanied. He imagined that the explanation was that the Mess Steward allowed them in to boost the takings. The bar was almost empty but the girls headed straight for them and asked if they could join them. "Of course," said Freddy "be our guests. Can we buy you a drink?" The girls both ordered the same gin and black after introducing themselves as Olga and Heidi. Olga was in her early twenties and she was a very attractive brunette. Her English was perfect and if one did not know any better was English and not German. Heidi was about the same age but she had a heavy accent and was far more reserved than Olga.

Olga sat close to Freddy whilst Heidi sat next to Pinky. Olga and Heidi told the boys that they had both been married but were now single again. No further information was given but Olga said that she had lived in London for many years before returning to her parents' home close to the airfield. "I am constantly interested in what is happening in England" She said. After a couple more drinks Olga said that she needed some air and asked Freddy to walk with her for a while. They went out through the accommodation entrance and Olga turned and led Freddy to the alcove next to the entrance. The alcove at one time had had a monument or statue housed there but it was now just a large semicircular, dark inlet. She pulled him closer to her and her arms wrapped around his neck drawing his lips into a demanding kiss. Her passionate sexual advances were just too much to resist and Freddy went along with her sexual demands. Freddy was taken by surprise but he did not resist as it had been some time since he had been on leave. She broke away, after the completed act, just as suddenly as she had started and she smoothed her dress and turned towards the door. She paused and looked back at Freddy just standing, watching her walk away. "I'll get the drinks in." she said and she walked into the bar.

Freddy adjusted his clothing and stood a while wondering what and why? He had never encountered anything like it but he was not complaining. He returned to the bar and Olga. She smiled at him and took a drink of her recently filled gin and black. They sat in a comfortable silence until the door of the Mess diner opened and Pinky emerged with Heidi. Obviously from the smile on his face, Pinky had experienced a similar time with Heidi. Heidi stopped to talk to the young barman before returning to the table. The girls quickly drank their drinks, thanking the boys as they left the Mess and said that they looked forward to the next time.

Freddy and Pinky looked at each other. "What an earth happened there? How did that happen? I've never had anything so matter of fact happen before. Olga did not seem to consider me at all. I think that I have just been taken advantage of, which was novel. I think that things may have taken a turn for the better if they are looking forward to seeing us, we'll have to come back here again. The mess was now deserted except for the boys. "The barman is trying to attract your attention. Have you paid your bar bill?" "Of course I have, I wonder what that 'Wallah' wants. I'll go and find out. You are right, I have never known anything like those two girls. Don't let anyone touch my drink." With that Pinky made his way to the bar and was in an intense conversation for some time before he returned. Freddy sat alone with his drink and mulled over the thoughts about what they were doing. It did seem an awful waste of resources flying the Varsity for just one day a week, even though they regularly extended their operation time.

"What seems to be the problem, Pinky?" Pinky took a deep drink, almost emptying a full lager glass of mainly gin combined with a splash of tonic. "He must have upset you for you destroy a drink like that, what is it?" Pinky took a deep breath, "He has just offered me all the fags and booze that I can manage for sale in Blighty. The price that he wants is 2d for a packet of Senior Service and a shilling for a bottle of Black Label whisky." "I don't believe it. We could make a fortune at those prices. Is it legal?" "Of course not, but I told him that we would talk to him next week and let him know. It means getting the stuff through Marham Customs and unloading without attracting attention back at base. We will have to look into developing a viable M.O. Think about it." "Where is he getting them from at those prices?" asked Freddy. "Best not to ask, let him deal with this end, we have enough on our hands with the logistics of distribution."

They stayed in the Sergeants mess until bedtime and any opportunity or thought of visiting the local town of Wildenrath was dampened by the weather. Following an uneventful return flight, the week dragged on until next Tuesday sortie to Germany. They had made discrete inquiries about demand for drink and cigarettes and they had found much interest and request for cheap supplies. "I've made all necessary arrangements but if you don't want to go ahead with this, I will call the whole thing off." said Pinky. "It is more than difficult to ignore the possibilities and the risks are not too bad, I'm sure that we can pull it off as long as we do not take too much each trip. We'll give it just one go and see what happens eh?" "Good lad, I've had a chat with a former associate at Marham and I don't see us having too much to worry about, operation 'Drag 'n' drink' is underway." said Pinky.

CHAPTER 3

As soon as they arrived in the mess in Germany, Pinky contacted Carl, the young barman, and told him that it was a go. Carl was about twenty something years old. He looked like a real country sort of boy but he was always enthusiastic and friendly to the Mess members. He was married with two daughters and lived locally near the R.A.F. station. He did not seem to be the type to organise and arrange such an operation but Carl said that he would the arrange loading after the bar closed later that night and Pinky said that they would meet him at 0030 hours to oversee everything and make sure that they had only what was needed. The boys spent the rest of the evening in the mess and as usual the girls arrived to entertain the boys.

It was a regular date for the boys now and they looked forward to their visits to the mess. The girls left early as usual but the boys stayed until the bar shut and then they went off to find their aircraft. Freddy and Pinky arrived just after midnight and the aircraft was already taking on its' cargo.

They both wondered how they got access to the plane when it was in the security area. Young Carl seemed to be very well connected. They boarded the aircraft to find that the fuselage was packed with an amazing amount of cigarettes and the flooring on the flight deck had been removed and packed with boxed bottles of black label whisky.

It was after 0200 hours before the flooring and fuselage panels had been replaced and on visual inspection nothing was unusual. The boys expressed concern over the excessive amount that had been loaded but Carl said that they need not pay for it until they sold it all back home. The boys thought that there was far too much but as they had planned a storage area at base which could take it all at a push, they did not make an issue of it. There was no paperwork for any of it and therefore they were not too upset about it.

Flight time was 0800 hours and after very little sleep the boys boarded and the aircraft took to the skies. They soon reached a height to leave the heavily clouded skies behind them and they flew over a mass of white fluffy cloud, it looked like a snow-covered landscape and solid enough to land on. During the war time there were fighter pilots who were so battle fatigued that they had perished trying to land on the clouds. The countryside below was totally covered until they reached the North Sea and they could see small fluffy clouds over a sparkling blue sea. Pinky was hoping that customs officer Jones was on duty at Marham but they were concerned and had a 'sweat on' all the way home. Freddy was even more disturbed at the rate of the fuel consumption. "How much extra weight are we carrying? We'll be flying on vapours soon." "Don't panic" said Pinky "we are about to coast in and we'll get some extra aviation fuel to get us back to base at Marham, I'm sure that officer Jones will help us."

"Anything to declare?" asked Jonesy. "We have a couple of packets of cigarettes and a couple of bottles of whisky." Pinky replied. Officer Jones looked at the log and gages, "You've used more fuel than usual, did you make any detours?" Freddy thought that the game was up but Pinky replied, "We hit a very strong headwind over France and our ground speed was about walking pace, we didn't think that we were going to make it." "The Met. Office got it wrong again eh? Let me stamp your contraband and we'll get you topped up to get you back to base."

They could not help smiling to each other as they got airborne again on the way back to base. "I told you 'Jonesy' was ok, mind you, I thought that it was going to get a bit awkward for a while but not to worry we are in the money, the lads will fall over themselves to buy at these prices." said Pinky. He had known Jones from years ago and he was always a little bit different from others on the course which is probably why he did not 'pass out' and failing the course.

There was something again that was different about him when Jones did his inspection but Pinky could not really put his finger on what it was.

Carl was absolutely right in that the stock went in just a few hours and the orders flooded in for the next delivery. The future was looking up and over the next few months they had made more money than they had ever done before. Their bank accounts were very healthy and the weekly supply sorties and visits with Heidi and Olga became a regular event and as Christmas approached demand went through the roof.

They looked forward to their visits to Germany but it was without warning that at that time that they hit their first problem. Loading was going well at the German airbase as usual and extra fuel was a standard procedure after the scare at Marham, "You will have a passenger with you this trip." said Carl. "What do you mean? You know that we are not allowed to carry passengers on service trips," said Pinky. "But you must!" said Carl. Carl looked very fearful and after a long pause the boys started to object but from out of the shadows a man suddenly appeared.

Carl physically reacted and stepped back to give a clear view of the intruder. He was a civilian of middle-eastern origin. He was a very large man and from his attitude he was not used to any argument. He was very reminiscent of the archetypal-American gangster villains of the film industry. He was wearing a wide pin stripe suit and two-coloured patent shoes and a large brimmed hat. A heavy black woollen coat was draped across his shoulders. "You have no choice about what we tell you, you are involved too deeply to have any qualms about such a small request. You will do as we ask without any unpleasantness." The abject fear on Carl's face sent a stark message to the boys and they looked at each other. Pinky was most concerned by Carl's reactions and knew that there was more to this than was immediately apparent.

A period of threatening silence followed, during which time the boys tried to weigh up the situation. It was broken when Pinky realised that the intruder was armed. "Well, I suppose that we could go along with it this time," said Pinky. He also realised that this was the thin end of the wedge and that they would be asked to do more and more and he resolved that this was the last trip to Germany on this supply run. Suddenly everything became clear, the cigarettes, the booze, Heidi and Olga, they had fallen into a honey trap and that this man who threatened them was obviously part of a larger powerful organisation. It suddenly became apparent how Carl had been able to set it all up with the boys. He would request the transfer for himself and his crew as soon as he got back, irrespective of the money that they would be giving up but this was just too serious to get involved any further. Both of the boys had seen the tell-

tale sign of a gun under that jacket of the stranger and although Freddy was ready to object, he bit his tongue and nodded his agreement to Pinky. "Very wise, we would not like to see you come to any harm over such a trivial matter," said the stranger. Carl audibly showed his relief at their consent and a sickly smile appeared on his face, "Can we complete the loading boss?" he asked. "Get on with it!" was the sharp reply and after a long stare at the boys the man quickly faded back into the shadows.

The rest of the crew were not present at this encounter and so they were totally unaware of any of the events involving the stock transfers and were a little puzzled by the conversation on the return flight. The crew was aware that the boys had hit a lucky streak as they had profited along with the boys but they could not help overhearing their conversation as the boys discussed with whom they had become involved', it was obvious that Carl was just a minion and the girls just an encouragement.

CHAPTER 4

Pinky was in the Wing Commanders office the first thing the next morning. Wing Commander Fotheringhall was a short and slightly fat individual and he was known to be petty and spiteful. He was not at all respected and he was mostly avoided by aircrew members. How he was ever promoted to his post was a mystery to all who knew him. It was the general belief that the man was so incompetent that station commanders had been pleased to move him on and up. "What is it James?" asked the Wing Commander. "I want to request my crew and I be transferred to another operations section Sir." "Out of the question Master Sergeant, I have specific orders that you are to remain on your present supply runs. These runs are too important to be allocated to an inexperienced replacement crew. We also need to find that so called second navigator that you picked up in Germany on your last trip. I gave no sanction for passengers and to top it all he seems to have gone A.W.O.L. Until this matter is concluded you are going nowhere. Do I make myself clear?" "But Sir" "That is all James." Pinky left his office feeling very confused about the response that he had experienced.

How did 'Fothers' know about the passenger? "How did it go?" asked Freddy. "It was very strange, he knew about our passenger and he told me that this supply flight is too important to hand over to another crew." "I don't get it, it's just a routine supply run, any crew could do it," said Freddy "what's so special about this run and how did he know about the passenger and as he does know, why aren't we on a fizzer?" "That's what puzzles me as well," said Pinky, "from the way he was talking I would guess that he knows everything about the flights, including the cargo, why isn't he letting on? We will just have to see what happens on the next run. I have a nasty feeling that it is not just us involved in this project, the information arrived too quickly for it to be coincidental and I don't really understand any of it."

The Tuesday trip without a hitch but as they landed on the return trip at Marham, the aircraft was diverted to a large hanger furthest away from the administration buildings. There was no explanation given but they found themselves directed to a customs office where Officer Jones was waiting for them. He sat behind a large desk and they were both seated opposite on chairs at a lower level than Jones facing the window. This was obviously designed to put the boys at a disadvantage. As they sat in the lower chairs facing the silhouette of Jones Pinky demanded "What's this all about Jones?".

Jones rose from his seat and bent down to lift a case of whisky onto the desk. The boys recognised the case as one of those loaded in Germany. Without a word, Jones ripped open the case and took out a plastic bag of white powder. "Drugs!" said Jones "You have been making waves boys and we do not appreciate you causing any problems for us. Ali warned you in Germany to get on with it without any sort of objection but you went to see your Wing Commander requesting a transfer. You are working for us and you do nothing unless we say so." The boys immediately realised why it had been so easy for them to bring in the cigarettes and whisky.

It became clear to Pinky the difference in Jones' attitude spotted on their last trip.

Not only was Jones involved but so was the Wing Commander and goodness knows who else. "How many of these cases have we brought in?" asked Pinky. "You have made plenty from your contraband goods but this is our little perk." said Jones. "You are all in on it and who else is with you?" asked Pinky and Jones replied, "It took you long enough to realise that but you don't have any idea how big or powerful our organisation is and it is now not for you to question. You will do exactly what you are told to do from now on, cross us and you will find yourselves shipped in boxes and dropped in a very deep hole. Your load will be dropped here this time and you will be transported back to your base by truck to pick up your gear. Is that absolutely clear? Your Germany routine is completed, you will be brought back here for your next flight. Do not attempt to speak to anyone but if they speak to you, you can tell them that you are on special duties. Do you understand?"

The boys nodded and then they were led out to a truck that was already loaded with their cargo. They climbed aboard and as they passed the guard room, the M.P.'s told them that they would see them soon, which was puzzling. They travelled back to base in complete silence but both were wondering what had happened to them over the last few months and they were both increasingly concerned about what the future held for them. It was obvious that they had been lured into a trap and the extent of that trap was now beginning to unfold.

As they drove up to their home base, they were stopped by the guards at the main gate and told to get out of the truck. As they climbed down they were greeted by a smirking Wing Commander Fotheringhall "Your transport will take you to your new quarters." and he pointed to a large black car. The boys' kit bags were being loaded into the boot. "You will enjoy your new posting seeing as you made the request." said the smirking Wing Commander and he turned and walked away. The boys regarded the Wing Commander with total contempt and anger knowing that he was an intricate part in their situation. The guards moved towards the boys and they were told to get into the car. The door was slammed shut and locked from the front seat of the car.

They were quickly driven away, escorted by a couple of motorcycle outriders. They had not been driving very long before the boys realised that they were heading straight back the way that they had come. The car left the Marham road as the car approached Upper Marham, turning off onto Burnthouse Drove Road and finally into Lady's Wood. Pinky recognised their immediate surroundings but had never been into the wood area. He looked at Freddy with apprehension and Freddy understood his disquiet. The car came to a halt outside of a long and high wall. The wall stretched as far as the boys could see while they sat in the car. On the opposite side of the road was a line of tall trees.

The driver got out of the car without speaking to them and joined one of the outriders on his motor bike. They rode off and were quickly out of sight. The boys sat alone in the car totally nonplussed and they wondered what was going to happen to them. They both thought of making a run for it but they thought that they were still locked in. Had they been able to get out they would not get far carrying their kit bags and they would not like to leave them. Suddenly the passenger door was opened by a middle-aged man. "Come on boys, get your gear and follow me. The man did not appear to be in the least bit like the aggressive guards and they felt a bit relieved that their fears may not be as expected. You can leave the car where it is, it will be taken care of."

The man headed for a large gate in the wall which swung open with very little effort and he headed for a very large house which was at the other side of a large quadrangle. "Come on lads!" said the man and the boys followed under the weight of their kit bags. Although the light was not good, they could see a manor house that had previously been the hub of a very large estate. The quadrangle was lined by buildings that looked like they had been developed for accommodation, including servant quarters and the lines of stables, some of which had been converted for other purposes but were instantly recognizable by the horse shoes above the doors, confirming their original purpose. There was a row of closed garages with large double doors but the gravelled area did not show any signs of recent activity. Grasses and other plants were gradually taking over the gravelled quadrangle.

The man led them across the quadrangle towards a wing of the manor house, through an open door and up some uncarpeted stairs. They were led to the top floor in the wing of the manor house where there were a number of self-contained flats. "This apparently is your posting for the time being, take any of the furnished flats here, whichever you want as there are no other residents at the moment. Breakfast is at 0630 hours. Young Tom will give you a morning call and show you the way to the kitchen." The man went downstairs leaving Freddy and Pinky to explore. They did a quick tour of the rooms. Large rooms had been divided into smaller areas and furnished for one or two people to occupy. All the rooms seemed to be approximately designed from a standard plan and were very basic but comfortable. Looking out of the windows they could see the rear gardens which were unkept but extensive. Lawns spread from the house with trees interspersed to give separate areas. They could a large expanse of woods in the distance.

Looking to the front they could see the quadrangle where they had arrived and woods over the high wall. They chose the two larger adjacent rooms closest to the staircase, dumped their kit bags and fell into bed.

Chapter 5

The boys both felt that they had just closed their eyes when Tom banged on their doors waking them for breakfast. Tom was a young, fresh-faced lad and though he did not talk much he seemed quite pleasant. He waited for them to wash and dress and then led them down a stair case that had once been used by staff. The staircase led straight into a large kitchen on the ground floor. The kitchen was large with an open stove that would take a whole hog on a spit. The irons were still in place. The stove had ovens heated by the fire in which food could be kept warm or cooked. There were a number of doors leading out of the kitchen, one of which led to the servants' quarters. That was the door that they had used. It was obvious that this had been a very important and very well staffed private estate at one time.

They sat at a large wooden table where a cook of days long gone would have prepared giant meals for those upstairs. They enjoyed a very hearty breakfast but as they ate, confused thoughts made it difficult to understand what had happened to them and what plans were in store for them. Why they were where they were made no sense to them whatsoever. They sat quietly drinking a cup of tea when the kitchen door opened to reveal the man from the shadows in Germany. He entered the kitchen. The boys just could not believe that this man was here in England. In the daylight they were confronted by a very large man.

He reminded Freddy of a Greek wrestler. He had a fleshy face but his appearance was that of a man of a very cruel nature. His mouth twisted as he spoke which made the sickly smile on his face quite grotesque. "My name is Ali Ishmail and I control all operations in this part of the world. You will no doubt have many questions but let me explain, you two no longer exist. All record of your existence has been erased from every record everywhere in the world. The rest of your crew have been split up and posted separately. You have been chosen to work for us. You will be given orders that will be obeyed without question. You will be given a few days to familiarise yourselves with our private aircraft and you will be operational in three days-time. Failure to comply will be fatal and failure is not an option. Is that perfectly clear? You now belong to us and you will do as you are told without question." The boys nodded in dismay. Ali turned and left the kitchen.

Freddy was first to break the silence, "This has to be some sick kind of joke. They can't get away with this kind of stuff in England." Pinky replied, "It looks as if they can do it and they have done it but the question is who are these people and what do they want with us? They must carry some clout if Ali is right. We must have become involved with a very powerful organization if they can wipe our service records, they must have control in some very high places. Do they belong to our security set up or some other? How can they wipe out our existence in records? We will just have to go along with it until we see how the land lies and what they have in mind for us."

At that, the door opened and Tom and the older man came in. "I am sorry that I could not introduce myself earlier but I was under instructions and they are not the sort of people that I would like to upset. My name is Alan and I own this place. We normally have groups staying with us but it is a quiet period at the moment and they have paid to hire the whole place so who am I to argue? They say that you will only be here for a short time, I'm not sure how long and they tell me that they will come for you by car when you are needed. You have the freedom of the manor but I have to warn you not to try to leave, they tell me that the consequences will not be pleasant, whatever that means. Tom and I will help you but we know nothing other than you are to stay with us a while, anything outside of that and we cannot help. They say that they are a Government Department but we don't really know who these people are. They have just paid well for your accommodation but we have been told not to discuss anything that we see with you. It's a funny-goings on but business is business. The pantry is well stocked and so is the bar next door. Help yourselves to anything that there is and you have the complete run of the place. Have a pleasant few days, boys." Alan left them with Tom. "What can you tell us about this

Tom?" said Freddy "and who is this Guy Ali?" "You heard what Alan said but I've never seen that fellow before, he is one of Alan's customers. I have heard Alan on the phone to him once or twice but Alan said that he would pay very good money to look after two men coming to visit for a few days. I was told to show you around and help you find what you wanted." "What does Alan do? I mean does he work?" asked Freddy. "I've never known Alan have a job, if that's what you mean.

I came here when I was very young, a baby in fact and I have never known my parents but Alan and his wife always have looked after me. The wife died years some ago from some illness. I was never told what illness. They have never been short of money so I think that they must have investments or something. I will have to go now I have some jobs to do, see you in a while crocodile." "Well, that wasn't much help was it but we do know that they are not part of whatever the plan is." said Pinky. "I don't like this at all and there is nothing we can do about it for a while, so I suppose that we will just have to sit tight, I just wish that I could get my hands on that Wing Commander." said Freddy. Pinky nodded his agreement.

The events of the next two days consisted of trips in the car to the Marham airfield and familiarisation with an aircraft that Pinky thought was Russian made but had English labelling on the instruments. It was quite alien to Pinky and it took quite a few hours to become familiar with all the controls. The navigation system was also new to Freddy who had never seen such a radar/radio communication system. The only vague comparison that they could make was to a DC3. All other times were spent back at the manor house where they saw very little of anyone else.

The manor was bigger than they had first thought and the grounds beyond the building were varied and extensive. Freddy walked alone through the grounds lost in his own little world. As he walked, he tried to imagine the estate in its' former glory. There must have been a considerable number of staff to keep the place going. From the portraits in the house, he imagined a well to do family walking the grounds, the ladies in long flowing dresses and the men in formal dress. The children were of course not allowed to be near the adult family and were probably being looked after by nannies or a house keeper. The grandeur of his thoughts cut out his present predicament for a while and he strolled through the ages in his thoughts. As he approached the manor house he was brought back to reality with a realisation of his and Pinky's situation. After they had had lunch in the kitchen both boys set of together to look around the estate and grounds.

As they walked, they were aware that they were being followed at a discreet distance by at least two men. Earlier Freddy had not been aware of any followers but he realised that he must have been observed by somebody. After a while, they forgot about their observers and wandered through the gardens and woods on the estate. They talked about the past events and how they had become involved in something that they could not understand but as they talked they understood that they had been targeted for some reason and purpose to the benefit of this strange organisation. They were on their guard but could not imagine what lay ahead of them.

They spent the best part of the next day eating and sleeping and though there was every alcoholic drink available to them, neither felt like drinking. On the second evening following, they were sat twiddling their thumbs and they were quite bored when the door burst open and Tom told them to pack their flying bags and be ready to leave early next morning. The kit bags could be left for the time being.

The next morning the boys were washed and dressed when Tom came to tell them that they were to leave in thirty minutes. There was just time to grab a bite to eat before the car came to take them to the airfield. Tom had already put their flying kit in the car while they ate. The boys asked the driver where they were going but they were told that they would find out when they got there. They drove the short distance and entered Marham airfield through a perimeter gate and the aircraft was parked within in hundred yards of the entrance.

CHAPTER 6

They boarded and were told to maintain radio silence, no contact with the control tower. They were given local F.I.R. settings and they prepared for take-off in their own time. A now familiar threatening voice told them that the heading was for West Berlin airfield and to maintain radio silence all the way. The F.I.R. details were displayed on the strange radar set and altered as they left each region. They did exactly as Ali told them. They were not alone on the flight-deck, two uniformed, armed guards watched them at all times. They were all on the same intercom so everybody could hear what was said. Only Pinky spoke to Ali saying that there was a Berlin blockade and they might be shot down when entering West Berlin. The intercommunication system stayed quiet, no response. The boys were unable to talk to each other without being overheard so the flight continued in silence. The flight over the North Sea was quite bumpy but as they coasted into France the weather became perfect flying conditions. The fields and farm houses were clearly in view as they flew over the countryside. They were both getting more unsettled with the situation, especially as they approached the West Berlin airfield. Suddenly the radio/radar system burst into life with landing instructions and the aircraft landed without challenge or approach by any sort of security. On landing Pinky was told to prepare for immediate take-off after refuelling. A tanker vehicle quickly linked up with the aircraft and soon completed the job of preparing the aircraft for take-off. They were ready to go when a small group of men ran across the airfield towards them. Pinky was told to wait for them to get on board. As soon as the hatch was closed, the order was given to take-off and head back to Marham. Pinky felt quite silly after he asked over the communication system what customs would make of this but he just felt that he had to say something. His comments were completely ignored and everything went without a hitch back to Marham.

The boys were driven back to the manor house and for the first time on arrival could speak freely. "I knew that we wouldn't be challenged on landing. Whoever or whatever this organization is they must have this place completely under their control." said Pinky. "That occurred to me as well but I also think that I know why we are here. They know that we know nothing about them so if we get caught on this mission, whatever it is, we can't tell anyone anything. I recognised a member of the party that got on board and that really does worry me. The leading runner was Fidel Castro, I would know him anywhere. It was either him or a very close double. I think that we are being used for a suicide mission." replied Freddy. Pinkys' mouth dropped open, "You surely can't be serious. Was that really Castro? Whatever is he doing over here?" "Whatever this operation is we are expendable and may not make it alive but if we succeed, we are definitely done for anyway. That's why our records have been destroyed," said Freddy "I think that we are in the proverbial Pinky." Pinky looked hard at Freddy and thought for a while, "I think that you are right. At least we know what we are up against so we need to be prepared for all eventualities. Watch for any opportunity that presents itself in the meantime don't let on that you suspect what they are up to. Especially don't let them know that you saw and recognised one of the passengers"

The boys sat around for the next few days, surprised that they were back at the manor house with very little sign of Tom over that time. They had tried to scale the wall to escape but each time they tried anything an armed guard appeared from nowhere. The guards were never in view and their stationing was a very well kept, secret. They were never in sight until an attempt to escape occurred. There had to be someone monitoring the gate at all times because each time they got close to it a guard would appear. They thought constantly about escape scenarios but even if they got away what could they do and where would they go without identities? In a world where they knew that officially they no longer existed. As they were having breakfast one morning Tom came and said "You have a night flight tonight, be ready to leave at 1800 hours." He turned and went out leaving the boys astounded at his actions. "That wasn't like Tom at all I've never seen him so agitated. The job must be on tonight, I wonder what they have in store for us?" said Freddy." "Well, Castro must still be around somewhere. They couldn't move him around the countryside without causing a stir of some sort. I wonder if our mission has something to do with him and transport out of the country to goodness knows where." replied Pinky. They both knew that this was crunch time and they had to be aware of any chance of getting away before the inevitable. They had to keep their wits about them it was now or never. The evening was overcast and it was quite dark but the wind was very light and a slight mist was developing. When the time came to go, two armed men took them by car to Marham airbase and straight to a waiting aircraft. The airfield was covered in slowly swirling mist which made long vision a bit of a lottery. As soon as they got on board Pinky whispered to Freddy that he had flown this very aircraft in nineteen forty-six just after the Second World War. It was one of five bought from the American Air Force and this is the one that he had to test fly. Now it was clear why they had been chosen. It was one of the first Constellation flight purchased before the Lockheed 049 fleet were bought. Pinky told Freddy that they must be in for a long journey and that Freddy must be correct in who they had picked up in

Berlin. One of the armed men ordered them to be silent and take up their positions. The passengers were boarding and the boys were now certain of their identities. Pinky said "This is it Freddy we have to look for any opportunity now that it is make or break, fingers crossed we get a chance."

    The intercommunications burst into life with instructions to take off in ten minutes on a heading of 270 degrees. Freddy put on his helmet and acknowledged. He thought on what Pinky had said and he was in better spirits than he had been in some time. As soon as they were in the air a course was set for due west and they settled down at cruise speed. The mist was quickly left behind as it was very close ground mist and it was clear after just a few feet of climb. They both knew that they were in for a long-haul flight and maintaining radio silence as usual. Freddy had to guess what the F.I.R. variations might be, so they continued their flight on direct vision and pure assessment of air pressures and conditions from previous meteorological forecasts. They were given more details of the flight plan as they flew across the Atlantic Ocean. Freddy realized that they were heading for America but was not sure why they were not taking the southern Atlantic crossing. It dawned on him that the Atlantic patrols would question their identity and may prove to become problematic. The northern route took much longer as the prevailing wind was head on and slowing their progress. They changed heading to 330 degrees and after some time landed at an airfield in Canada for refuelling and then set a course due south. As they flew across American air space, they were occasionally investigated by military aircraft but they didn't come under any pressure from them as they were recognised as an American made aircraft. The outer insignia had not been clear on previous viewing so neither of the boys knew of any recognition marks. They were allowed to fly on unimpeded. They landed twice more for refuelling. Pinky thought that the final filling wasn't necessary but each time they landed they took on more equipment. Pinky realised that the extra weight was the need to take on more fuel. At last, he was informed of the destination and to his amazement he learned that it was San Julian Air Base in Cuba. On landing the extent of the cargo unloaded was far more than either of the boys had imagined. They saw everyone disembark except the two-armed guards and Freddy tried the flight deck door "We are still locked in here." At that the door opened and one of the guards ordered them to take off straight away on a heading of 310 degrees. The door was closed as the guard left but noticeably not locked. The aircraft took off on the prescribed heading. The intercom. had been silent even before take-off, which was unusual, so after thinking about it for a few minutes Pinky set the auto pilot as he was aware that they were heading back into American air space. Pinky ventured through the unlocked door and disappeared for a while only to return very excited "There is no one on board except us. I've checked everywhere." "Great then let's take this baby home." said Freddy. Pinky took the controls and tried to manoeuvre but the controls had been remotely locked by a timing device. They were coasting in to mainland America heading in a direction for Oklahoma or Kansas. "I have no control the auto pilot will not turn off and I can't do a thing about it. I have no idea how they have jammed all the controls." exclaimed Pinky. Pinky carried on "By the time I find out what it is that they have done we will have run out of fuel and headed for the deck." They both abandoned their positions and searched the aircraft looking for parachutes but all they found was a load of papers in a hold-all. They thought that were completely trapped when it occurred to Pinky "We always kept spare chutes under your navigation position when I flew this crate last. Freddy, go and see if you can still find them." Freddy returned a little later wearing a parachute and he handed another to Pinky who quickly put it on. "All this paperwork is in Russian and it looks as if we have become traitors helping this lot. I will keep this stuff for future use because it might be helpful to prove that we are not spies." Pinky stuffed the paperwork and two large envelopes into his flying suit having checked one and found some American Bonds in there. He hoped that they might be as good as cash if and when they were needed. They went to open the doors to escape but found all of the exits had been sealed shut. They were trapped. It occurred to Pinky that the navigation loading bay door might have been overlooked and so they set off back to the flight deck and dropped into the navigation bay door space. This door also seemed to be sealed. They sat there in despair for a few minutes and they were chilled to hear the aircraft engine noise change. "We must be flying on vapours." said Pinky and in pure frustration he kicked out at the navigation bay door which burst open taking the boys by surprise. The boys found themselves in space falling out from beneath the navigation position. The doors had burst open and they had fallen out under the aircraft. They deployed their parachutes as quickly as they could which was a mistake as they were above ten thousand feet and without oxygen and they both felt quite light headed in such low oxygen levels. Their breathing soon returned to normal as they descended and their spirits rose at their unexpected freedom. They descended through sun warmed space in a very light breeze. They started to enjoy the descent and the view of the landscape below and the large town which was not too far from where they would land. They were shocked out of their thoughts by a loud explosion and they saw bits of the Constellation and black smoke drifting towards the earth. They both realised that they had just made it out of the aircraft in time. Ali and friends had taken every conceivable opportunity to make sure that the boys did not survive. As they drifted to the ground Freddy took notice of the area below them. They were heading very close to a road below that appeared to head for a very large town to the west of their position. Before the road reached the town there was a small village on the same road. They both came to ground safely and quickly disposed of their parachutes, hiding them well out of sight in a wooded area. Freddy said, "We need to get out of our flying suits, we would be very conspicuous in them. We have shirt and trousers that will more fit the bill in this part of the U.S.A." Remembering the direction of the large town seen from the air they soon made it to a highway and headed towards town. As they walked, they discussed their lucky escape and wondered if they would be thought of as now dead by their captors. They concluded that that would be the best outcome as long as they could stay undetected by any of the authorities. They had been walking for quite a while when an old truck approached from behind them. Freddy thumbed a list and to their relief the truck came to a halt beside them. "Howdy boys you headed for town?" came the question from the driver. "We are aiming for the town up the road." The driver told them to jump up onto the back of the truck. They thanked the driver and climbed aboard. As they were travelling Pinky had a good look at the bonds in the envelope from the aircraft and was astounded to find about fifty, ten thousand American dollar bonds, "We will have to risk trying to cash one or two of these bonds. We haven't any money on us and we can't get very far without some collateral. If there is a Bank of America in Dallas, we will try there'. They had just passed a road sign directing them to Dallas which showed that Pinky's navigation skills were not what he imagined. They passed through the small hamlet which was called Kaufman and soon arrived in the outskirts of Dallas. The driver with a goodbye wave let them get out of the truck in the banking district which was a very welcome and an unexpected coincidence. It did not take long to find a Bank of America and they offered one of the bonds to the cashier. After a long look at them and the bond, the cashier handed over the cash without further question. As soon as they left the bank they divided the money so that were both independent and could manage if they were separated. They agreed that they would need transport as a priority and headed for a car dealer that they passed on the road as they got to the banking district. They walked along the road towards the car dealer's place but the Dallas that they had seen on TV and films was nothing like what they now experienced. They passed crowds of Americans but nobody gave them a second glance and they soon began to relax and felt that maybe their ordeal was at last over. For just a couple of hundred dollars they drove away from the garage with a full tank of petrol in a nearly new Chevrolet convertible. Freddy said "We need to get as far away from here as fast as we can. We need as much distance between the wreckage of that aircraft and us as we can get. It is sure to be reported on the radio and people just might connect us as strangers to the event. What is the best direction for us to take?" Pinky replied "I worked with a young American pilot on the aircraft transfers in 1946 and he lived and worked in Washington D.C. so I think that that is our best bet. I am sure that he will remember me and I am sure that he will help us to get out of this mess." They headed on route thirty towards Arkansas and onto route sixty-six. Freddy was fairly familiar with American maps and knew that once on route sixty-six Washington signs were easy to follow. "I'm glad that you know where you are going, I wouldn't have a clue." said Pinky remembering his previous destination estimate. They shared the driving knowing that it would take hours and hours to reach Washington especially as they would need to stop for a rest somewhere on route. It had been many hours since they had had any sleep and night flights do take a toll on concentration. They were both getting very tired and they had frequent stops to avoid falling asleep and to stretch their legs. In consequence it took far longer than it should have done to reach Texarkana where they stopped and booked a couple of rooms at a motel on west 9th street. It was a rundown boarding house rather than a motel but the owners made an effort to keep the place clean and tidy. The sheets were fresh and clean and felt so welcome after their journeys. They fell asleep as soon as they lay down on their beds. They had booked a morning call but they were both up and dressed before the call came. The owner was very inquisitive about two 'Limies' staying at his place but they said that they were just touring. After a hearty breakfast they made enquiries about the nearest Bank of America and were outside the bank as the door opened. The owner had been very insistent on the boys talking about themselves and how they had acquired Bank America accounts. They hastened off to the bank as soon as they could get away. Without any problem they each cashed two bonds and left the bank. Once outside they got into the Chevrolet and headed on route sixty-six to Arkansas. The journey was very pleasant, Freddy had not travelled the roads of America before and he found that it was quite relaxing compared with U.K travel. They made it to Little Rock, Arkansas in good time and went straight to the bank and cashed another two bonds each. The bank clerk looked at them in an inquiring way but did not hesitate in cashing the bonds. They now had plenty of money in case of any emergencies that might occur.

  They decided to take a break and spent the afternoon and evening taking in the sights of the city which relaxed them before bed. They came across the Arkansas Arts Centre located on the corner of 9th and Commerce streets in MacArthur Park there was lots of activity and a lot of development work was going on. One of the people watching struck up a conversation with the boys. He was very interested in their accents and where they came from. He thought that he had ancestors in the U.K. and wondered if they knew of his family, the Browns, who he thought lived near London, England. The boys told him that they lived a lot further north and could not help. Jed had been born in Little Rock and was proud to explain that the town Mayor was leading a group of developers upgrading and expanding the Arts Centre. They thanked Jed and set off to explore further. As they walked, they wondered if they had been wise telling Jed about themselves but decided that he seemed genuine enough and they stopped worrying about their meeting.

The next morning, they left Little Rock, Arkansas and headed on to the next big town but when they tried to cash more bonds they met a problem. The cashier was presented with the bonds but he headed for the back office only to return with a blank refusal to pay out. He asked them to accompany him to the office. The boys demanded the return of the bonds and promptly left. They realised that the banks had been alerted and they left town as quickly as possible aware now that their previous captors knew that they had somehow escaped their trap and were still alive. How they had got the information to the bank and its' staff amazed them. They hit the road again and headed non-stop for Washington D.C. After some consideration they concluded that; "It was obvious really that if we kept drawing money it would soon register with their organisation that we had the bonds from the aircraft." said Pinky. "We had no choice Pinky," said Freddy "They are not stupid these people, whoever they are and they must keep account of their finances. They would soon realise that we or someone else was cashing the bonds left on the Constellation, in fact, they knew that if we survived it was likely that we would find them and spend them.

In fact, it might have been a follow up trap. They will now know our heading by the trail that we left. We need to get any help from your friend as quickly as possible. They might already be on our tails." The journey was taking more time than they had accounted for and the distances were greater than first thought. They continued their journey, sleeping alternately as the other drove the car.

Back in England Charlie King addressed the airmen gathered together in Hilarys' cafe, Aunt Sally's in Bedale. It was the best eater near the air bases where they were all based. "Look lads, we have waited long enough for Freddy and Pinky to get here for this reunion. Does anybody know where they have been posted? I sent invitations to our last base and asked them to post them on. I can't see any of our old crew missing out on a reunion. Yvonne, have you seen any of the boys lately?" Yvonne replied that she hadn't seen anyone since the last meeting at the cafe. Jack the radio operator said "I tried to contact them through records but it was very strange because they said that they had no records of either of them. I couldn't find any trace of them being on operations with us either which is crazy." Charlie looked around the group, they were all very quiet. "Has no one heard from them?" There was no response. "Well lads, something is very wrong here has anyone asked around?" Roger said that he had been in touch with his very good friend, Jane in administration and she said that she would get back to him with any news of Freddy or Pinky. She had not been in touch at all. When he had phoned back to ask her again someone else answered and when he asked for Jane, he was told that he must be mistaken, there was no Jane in admin. "What the hell is going on here?" said Charlie "look lads we need to get to the bottom of this. Cubby, you have a high up relation in the M.O.D. can you contact him and make some discreet enquiries? The rest of you find out what you can and we will meet back here next week at the same time. I don't like the sound of all this so be as discreet as you can and do everything that you can lads." Before he left, he spoke to Hilary and told her how worried they all were and checking that she was happy about them having the upstairs room next week.

Cubby got a weekend pass as soon as he got back and took the first available train to London. He had contacted his cousin who held a high office in the Ministry of Defence and arranged to stay with him over the next two days. He arrived at King's Cross and he took the Green Line underground train to Gloucester Road station. He arrived at Petersham Place late in the evening to be greeted by his cousin Godfrey Bellinger. Petersham Place was a select location not far from Kensington Palace. The white painted houses were very expensive to upkeep but they were most sort after by those who could afford. The interior was very sparsely furnished and decorated but it contained all the essentials that a bachelor would need. Cubby was quite surprised how Spartan Godfrey lived but he sipped his gin and tonic and chatted to Godfrey about all the latest family news. Godfrey appeared to be very interested as he had very little contact with any of the family members. Godfrey worked in circles that were familiar to him but far removed from the normal life of the family. "Well old chap," said Godfrey "I'm sure that you didn't travel all this way just to chat about Aunty Elaine and the rest, what's the problem?" Cubby told him about the crew and the reunion and the fact that Freddy and Pinky had completely disappeared. He told him about their enquiries being blocked, stonewalled and being told that people they know had never worked at places where they had recently been contacted.

"Goodness gracious," exclaimed Godfrey "if what you say is true then it would appear that we have one almighty security problem. From what you say, I wonder who can we trust? There appears to be some corruption in your services. We will have a look and see what we can find out. We need to find your chaps without delay and gather all the information that we can. Leave it with me. My friend in security will know exactly what to do." Cubby was startled when Godfrey jumped up and said that he was off to see his security chap. He appeared not deterred by the fact that it was Friday evening and much of the ministry would be empty. Godfrey left the house at Petersham Place and headed for the ministry office, having informed Sir George Curswell that he was on his way. Cubby was left at Godfrey's house with instructions to stay as long as he wished so he went for a discovery tour of the house and then settled down for a relaxing evening with access to Godfrey's bar.

Sir George was waiting in his office for Godfrey to arrive, "What's the flap Godfrey? I am not very happy about having my Friday night interrupted. I do hope that it is something important that you have to report." "We may have a major security breach on our hands old chap." Godfrey went on to explain what had happened and how Cubby had come to see him with his story. "My goodness we can't have chaps disappearing without trace or record. Are you sure that this is not some kind of prank?" replied Sir George. "Cubby is a very reliable young man and I wouldn't doubt that he was deadly serious but it can't be too serious, it may just be down to forces records." said Godfrey. Sir George sat silent for a few minutes and looked very serious. "This is just incredible. I have been working through the implications of what you have described, we must find these chaps. The corruption must be extensive in more than one of our government departments. service records haven't got the power to mess with data. Who can we trust? Leave this with me overnight. I will meet you at nine tomorrow morning at the usual Green Park rendezvous." Godfrey was now questioning if it was wise to involve Sir George, it might blow up into something serious. Godfrey decided to stay over in town at the Union Club at St' James for the night so that he would be close to the morning rendezvous. He was a club member and the rooms were very comfortable and the food was excellent. He spent the evening dining and chatting in the bar lounge where service was very attentive. Godfrey arrived early next morning but saw Sir George already waiting for him. "At last Godfrey," as if he was suggesting that he was late, "I conducted a little investigation of my own last night and your cousin was correct. I could not find any record of the chaps that you mentioned. It looks as if we will have to be very careful who we trust in command in the services and in the ministry departments. We need an independent operative who knows his onions. We need someone who is anonymous. We have used a trusted agent on previous occasions called Huntley Haverstock. Very few people would know him. We always contact him through the Times advertising. We can't be seen to be involved in any investigation as it may alert whoever is behind all this. I will appoint Huntley and get him to contact you at the Petersham house and you will liaise directly with me, if that is alright with you? You will have to inform your guest that you have taken steps to find out what's happened and you will keep him in the picture" Godfrey nodded and they parted. As Godfrey travelled back to his house, he felt that he had opened a can of worms that would disturb his comfortable life style and arrived home feeling quite disturbed. Sir George went back to his office and contacted the Sunday Times to insert an advertisement for Huntley under the

Harley Davison code contact. He checked the file on Huntley and he was reassured that he had chosen well.

In the North East of England in a local rugby club, Tony Grey was enjoying lunch with his wife Rosemary when Barney came to their table. "Hey Tony, this is right up your street. You answered one of these advertisements about a Harley Davison bike before but you didn't get one. There is another special Harley for sale here." Barney handed the paper to Tony. Tony got up and with Rosemary they left straight away, leaving Barney wondering what he had said. Tony contacted the advertisement telephone number saying that he was interested in the Harley Davison background chart. The code was immediately recognised by Sir George "Is that you Huntley?" Tony confirmed giving the code response. "You are needed at once at the Petersham house without delay." The telephone line went quiet and the call was ended.

Huntley Haverstock arrived early Monday morning at Petersham Place. He dismounted from his Ducati motorcycle and parked it outside Godfrey's house. He didn't remove his helmet after ringing the doorbell. Codes were exchanged and Huntley was invited into the house. Godfrey didn't speak but handed Huntley a package and a letter of introduction to the Union Club in St. James. Nothing further was said and Huntley left and headed for the St. James club. He was shown to a room whilst a footman parked Huntley's Ducati in a secure area. When he settled into his room Huntley read the file containing information and instructions to investigate the disappearance of two airmen. He must conduct the investigation at all times in total secrecy. Money, security I.D. and passes were included in the package. He read the file over and over in complete disbelief at the possible corruption and the possibility that there was foreign infiltration into Government departments and armed forces. Sir George had made extensive enquiries and found that many more departments had been involved in this mystery. After his long journey Huntley decided to take time for a rest and then set off for Marham air base. He turned on the radio to hear the national news broadcast and was shocked to hear that a worldwide crisis was being reported. The newsreader reported that Cuba had begun to install Russian missiles at their air bases and was creating a threat against the U.S.A. No one knew how the missiles arrived there as the U.S.A. military monitored all traffic in and out of Cuba, it was a mystery. American officials were expressing their anger about the threatening Communist presence so close to their shores and there was talk of war. People around the world were talking about four- minute warnings and everyone was fearful of another world war. Later that day Huntley set off for Marham. As Huntley was leaving the club he noticed a man sitting in an overcoat in the very well heated Union Club lounge. Huntley was on the alert and as he rode away along Pall Mall. He saw a black Bentley car following and matching his speeds. To check that he was not imagining things he made a quick detour and the Bentley followed. Huntley stopped at a news agents shop and watched as the Bentley kept on going past. He headed out of London on the road to Marham. It came as a shock when he saw the same Bentley car about four hundred yards behind him again matching his speed. He turned into the first café and lorry stop that was familiar to him along the road. He parked the Ducati out of sight at the rear of the cafe and went in through the cafe front door. As he entered the door, he saw the Bentley turn in and park. Three of the Bentley occupants followed him into the cafe. Huntley made sure that they heard him order a full English breakfast with a mug of tea. He took his breakfast, which he certainly did not need after the club breakfast and sat down at a table close to the toilet door. He placed the food on the table and sat down. He had a good view of the service counter and the rest of the tables. He discreetly watched as the trio took a table by the front door. After a minute or two Huntley got up and stretched leisurely and leaving his breakfast untouched on the table he strolled into the toilet. Quickly he left the building through the toilet window and started his bike and headed up the farm path at the side of the cafe that he had noticed as he arrived. He had seen a wooded area further up the path and made for it knowing that any followers would have to be on foot. He hid in the woods and it wasn't long before he saw his followers running around looking for him or his bike. They eventually went back to the car and turned in the direction of Marham, assuming that Huntley had resumed his journey. Huntley planned a route away from main the roads, it would take a little longer but it would be much safer. He wondered if his followers were standard surveillance or was his mission already compromised. Huntley remembered his R.A.F. service years in air traffic control and as he approached Marham he considered those who may still be serving here in Customs and air traffic control. He quickly contacted those he had served with and who were still there in both groups and took a risk of carefully questioning those members that he considered most reliable.

Although no one knew anything specific Huntley put together the information and came up with a revealing account of the events of the night Constellation flight and its' aircrew. Having offered his thanks and goodbyes Huntley set off to go straight back to London. On his return journey he took particular care to check for any followers and he arrived back to the Union Club without any further incident. From the club he contacted Godfrey and made arrangements to pass all his information over to him. Godfrey told him to stand by for further instructions and then contacted Sir George and relayed the information to him. Sir George called together his most trusted agents but before the meeting he checked with the Air Traffic Security Team. They had discovered a secret flight that had left the U.K. air space flown by a crew of whom they had been unable to find any record. The crew may not have been willing parties to the flight from information received but the crew need to be found without delay. This looked like a serious security breach and they were waiting for the F.B.I response for possible destinations on the American continent. Sir George addressed his agents giving them the information received from Air Traffic security and he continued, "As soon as I have any more news, I will forward it through the usual channels set up for red code one. The crew could be anywhere by now but I want those men found and brought here." The agents dispersed with the knowledge that this was a top priority mission.

The U.S. Secret service was concentrating on the same mission they had known about an aircraft explosion in American air space but it had not been thought to be significant at the time. The information from British sources changed all that and it was now a top priority. The proximity of the exploding aircraft to Cuban air space rang alarm bells at the Whitehouse. Priority instructions were given to all agencies to find the

Constellation crew assuming they were still alive. It was soon confirmed, with all the new information, that an aircraft had left American air space bound for Cuba and on returning, exploded near Dallas Texas. The search and investigation was now active.

Freddy and Pinky sat in a motel stunned by the news of the Cuban crisis. They now knew that they had been used in connection with the cause of the crisis but the extent to which they weren't sure as they were not sure what cargo they had carried. They had not been able to contact the friend in Washington D.C.

They had to leave when things became uncomfortable when they asked the whereabouts of the friend. They thought that unnecessary questions about their identities were being made and they suspected that they were being monitored in their enquiries. It was confirmed when they realised that they were being followed by two motorcycle outriders on the highway. They had left the highway as soon as an opportunity to leave the main roads presented itself. The roads were narrow and twisting as they made their way through the American back roads. They were unsure from time to time about their exact position and sometimes they were not certain of their heading. The roads that they were on made their way through tree lined avenues and meandered from south to north on occasions. The terrain changed so quickly from the familiar to the most unfamiliar. They were aware that they were on route 56 but were relieved that at last they knew where they were. They arrived at Middleburg and left the main street where off the main highway they changed the car and replaced it with a pickup truck and made their way to a small motel on W. Federal Street. As they sat in one of the rooms Pinky exclaimed "How did we let ourselves get involved in all this? I don't know what to do now. They are going to keep on hounding us until they catch us and kill us." The sound of a fast car approaching and then braking rapidly set their nerves on edge. Doors crashed open and loud voices could be heard as if from all directions. The boys froze. There was a tremendous crash as the door next to their room was broken down and shots were fired into the room. They thought that they had been chased to this motel and they feared that it would be their room next. They heard the sound of people running and all went quiet. They sat still, hardly breathing, when a knock came at their door. They thought it better not to open it but the voice of the desk clerk called them by name. Freddy opened the door and was greeted by the white-faced clerk who asked if they were okay. He went on to say that two gang members had been gunned down in the room next door after a shoot- out. He was glad to hear that the boys had not been harmed. The gangsters were known to him as they had demanded protection money from the motel takings so he wasn't too upset at the outcome of the incident. The boys were relieved to know that they were innocent bystanders in this incident but they realized that it could very well have been their pursuers after them. Freddy suggested, "We have got to stay off the main roads and keep going. I know of a place in the Catskills near Monticello where no one will find us. It is up in the state of New York so it is quite a ride to get there but I think we will be quite safe. The place used to be a summer camp for New Yorkers and mainly used by the Jewish children. I was once offered an exchange job there during the school holidays and the reports were very good. We will have to avoid the main highways so it will take us longer to get there but once there we can lay low as long as we need. The guy who used to own it went burst some time ago. We have the money and we can buy enough supplies to stay there indefinitely." "Good idea," said Pinky "if we travel by night and sleep during the day we will have more of a chance of making it." The rest of the day was spent looking around the area. They found a very pleasant eating place called 'Fat Boys' which supplied them with an excellent meal for a very reasonable price. They stayed at the motel until dark and then set off north heading for New York State. It was slow progress on the back roads, twisting and turning back and forth and as they travelled through the night. It was taking them far more time to make progress and they were forced onto the main highway by merging roads but two nights later they made it to route seventeen off route 87 and 6 before it was light. They travelled on and approached Ramsey

Motel just before the sun was up. They were physically and mentally exhausted and when they got to their rooms, they were asleep in no time and slept until late afternoon. They were wakened by the sound of heavy vehicles passing the motel. They made enquiries at the desk by phone but the reception could not help, other than to say that it was most unusual to have such traffic. They dismissed the occurrence as possible circus traffic. They had heard that the U.S.A. was keen on small town circuses. They freshened up and left the motel as the light was fading heading for Monticello and relative safety. The idea of getting there made them feel a little more relaxed and the plan to lay low there gave them a bit more confidence that things would somehow get better. On the smaller roads traffic was very light so they cruised along in good spirits even though it was getting quite dark and overcast. They passed abandoned houses on the forest roads where people had just moved on a little further up the road and built another house. It was quite strange for the boys to understand. It was most unlike any British idea. Suddenly a couple of miles up ahead of them Freddy saw some very bright stationery lights. Freddy asked "Do you think that it is a road block ahead?" Pinky agreed and they decided to turn around and try and find another way to their destination. Before they had a chance to turn around, they spotted some motorcycle outriders coming up fast behind them, followed by a very fast large vehicle. The riders were very familiar to them and they knew immediately that Ali's men had found them. Just as they spotted their pursuers shots rang out and the rear pickup window glass exploded into thousands of pieces covering them both with shards of glass. Freddy accelerated but they both knew that they could not outrun them. More shots hit the rear of the truck and as they were approaching the road block their attention turned to what was ahead but then there was a loud explosion just behind them.

"We've had it," said Freddy "they've got rockets." Fear gripped them both and they knew that there was nowhere for them to turn or avoid their pursuers. Pinky looked to the rear of them and saw that the explosion was close behind them. As he watched, the smoke and debris cleared behind them to reveal a clear road except for bits of debris that were the remains of their followers and their vehicles. It was then that an American fighter plane flew overhead and tipped its' wings in a victory salute. They had no idea what had exactly happened as the Military Police stopped just ahead of them and an armoured car circled and approached them from behind. They were trapped and the boys sat rigid expecting the worst as the Military Police came to the pickup truck. They could not be sure that these police were not in the pay of their pursuers. "Goodchild and James I presume?" the M.P. in charge continued, "You will follow us to New York. There are some people there just dying to meet you." The boys were stunned. Who was waiting to meet them? Could it be the Russian agents? If it was, they knew that their lifespan was now seriously limited. They had almost made it to relative safety only to be caught at the last moment. They turned their vehicle round and set off back up the road hemmed in by Police vehicles. They travelled along the tree lined back roads of New York State and all looked so tranquil and peaceful. Before they got to the city of New York the convoy turned onto another tree lined road and travelled for a few miles until they arrived at a security base. The road barriers were manned by armed guards which did nothing to ease the boys' concerns. They were taken into a large administration building and shown into a spacious room furnished with tables and chairs and loungers. The room reminded Freddy of the N.A.A.F.I. back home. He could not help but feel that he would love to be back in that N.A.A.F.I. again now. The M.P. ordered them to sit, "You're going be here for some time guys, so make yourselves comfortable." Armed guards stood at both ends of the room and all of the windows were barred so there was no chance of getting out. Neither of the boys felt immediately threatened so the idea of escape did not particularly appeal to them. The room was obviously used as a rest room and eating place for a large number of service people but from what the boys had observed as they arrived, a large number of people were no longer based at this unit. It must have been an air force or army base before its' present use. They lounged around and dozed from time to time during the twelve hours of waiting. During their wait they had been well fed and watered by service cooks. The food was very pleasant and there was plenty of it. They ate in silence and it was obvious to Freddy that Pinky was showing real signs of fatigue. He had never seen Pinky looking so tired and stressed. Pinky was renowned for his resilience in the face of any adversity. M.P.'s arrived to take Pinky out of the room leaving Freddy alone and feeling very apprehensive. His feeling did not last very long as minutes later the same thing happened to Freddy. He was taken along a series of corridors and shown into room which was furnished and had plush carpet from wall to wall. Sir George was in the room with some of his agents along with a lot of American top brass. Freddy had never seen such a display of scrambled egg and shiny medals. They sat at a very large polished table which reminded him of a court sitting in judgment. He had never been in a court room but he imagined that it must be like this. Was this the final act before they interrogated and then shot him? Freddy sat on a chair in the centre of the room facing them, not knowing how to cope with the situation and not knowing if they were friend or foe. The interrogators were not aggressive and they introduced themselves one by one and Freddy hoped against hope that these were the good guys and not his pursuers. They were all of respected official rank and they looked genuine but were they on the right side? He was asked his name, rank and number which he nervously gave them. Sir George started proceedings, "Relax Sergent Goodchild, your foreign pursuers have been dealt with. The officers here just need to know what happened to you following your last supply trip to Germany." Freddy was not fully convinced, "How do I know that I can trust you?" "You have no choice Goodchild you must be aware that you do not exist and all records of you have been destroyed. We need to know if you were a willing party to this unfortunate and damaging series of events." Freddy thought for a while and realised the implications of what Sir George had just said and he was right he had nothing to lose. He looked at the panel of interrogators in front of him and there was a look of sheer disbelief as he started to relate the recent events. It took a long time to relate the story of all that had happened to him and his friend but at the end of it the shock and surprise on the faces of his interrogators was a picture to see. His explanation was so comprehensive that there were no questions or challenges, everyone present was stunned by his story.

It was clear to all that the boys were totally innocent in the Cuban situation and had been forced to fly the aircraft with their cargo unwillingly. After reassurance by Sir George that they were not to be held at this base for long, Freddy was taken back to the room and Pinky joined him minutes later. When they were together again, they realized that the wait had been some time because people had flown from England to find out how seriously the boys were involved. They were there nearly another hour during which time they discussed the sessions that they had just experienced and their thoughts on the outcomes. They were now both relieved to feel that they were in friendly hands and they felt more relaxed than they had been for some time. Sir George entered the room "Come on chaps, it's time for you to go home. You've had one hell of an experience and we don't want any delay in getting you both back home." They were taken by car to the city and driven directly onto the airfield where they took off from New York Idlewild Airport in a private Trans-Atlantic jet.

On the journey to the U.K. Sir George explained seriousness of the awkward situation that had emerged since their kidnapping and the discovery of the Cuban crisis. The implications of the events that involved them and their erasure from all personnel records and other records were very worrying. He explained that their understanding of it was the distinct possibly that there had been extensive infiltration of foreign agents into all Government agencies and therefore trust and reliability was undermined throughout the whole of the Government services. He told them that for safety reasons they were to stay with a trusted friend of Sir Georges' called Godfrey Bellinger who lived at Petersham Place in London. Godfrey was a long-standing friend of Sir George and had come highly recommended as a trustworthy official. They were to stay at Petersham Place until further notice. He also informed them that members of their old aircrew had been very worried about them and instigated the search for them and it looked as if they owed their lives to them. It started to strike home to the boys just how close they were to death and it was only the timely intervention of the joint security services and American military that had saved their lives. The thought of their pursuers firing on them was fresh in their minds. 'Will the news of the U.S. Airforce taking out our pursuers be in the newspapers?" Asked Freddy. Sir George assured them that no one would be aware of the event, all news will be subject to a 'D' notice. They travelled nearly all the way in stunned silence, occasionally seeing the white tops of the waves in the Atlantic Ocean as they gazed out of the cabin windows. Knowing that they were now in safe hands and relatively safe did the shock really set in. The aircraft was no ordinary passenger plane, it had fully reclining seats, wide and very comfortable. It was fitted with a cafe and bar and carpeted cabin with lots of space to walk about. It appeared to be a very comfortable large lounge in the air. Tiredness overtook them both and they slept most of the way back to England. Freddy slipped into a sleep full of confusion and disturbing dreams. Foremost in his dreaming was the continuous pursuit and the outriders were disproportionate in size and threat they dominated the many types of pursuers who were mostly shadows flitting throughout his ethereal pictures. His memories pleasantly interrupted the pursuit of the outriders when he recalled his uncle Derek buying his first motor bike. Derek came to his home in Park Lane to show off his 500cc BSA. He offered to take Freddy for a ride and asked him to get his wellies for the ride. It was autumn and the conker season, so Derek headed for a local river at Stokesley in Cleveland where the banks were lined with horse chestnut trees. A few conkers lay on the floor but many had been stood on or partially eaten by the wild life. The best lay in the shallow stream in the river, so Derek encouraged Freddy to go into the water to recover them. Freddy had his wellies on so all would be well, or so Freddy thought. As he stepped into the fiver the water was only half way up his wellies but as he tried to pick up the conkers the water rose and filled them with cold water. He travelled home with pockets full of conkers and his wellies containing soggy feet. In his disturbed dream the water rose above his wellies up to his waist, then chest, then above his head and Freddy woke in a panic. They were both relieved to see the coast of England and as they coasted in to land some of the tension lifted. The sight of the green fields and hamlets of the

English countryside were pleasing to see and a wave of relief filled both Freddy and Pinky. They were driven quickly away from the airport heading for Godfrey Bellinger's house. Godfrey gave them a welcome and he seemed so relieved to see them, though he had never met either of them before. It was good to be back in England. They had a light supper and Godfrey was very interested in hearing their story while they ate. They soon were shown their rooms after telling Godfrey of their journey and they quickly retired for the night. They felt so refreshed after a good night's sleep. They had just finished breakfast when a car arrived to take them to see Sir George. As they travelled through the London city streets Freddy felt that they were being followed by a large black car. He thought that it must be his imagination and he put it down to his obsession with past events. Although he tried, Freddy could not shake off the feeling that they were still under surveillance by somebody. They arrived at

Sir George's office and they were admitted by an aide straight away. "Good morning chaps we have had some of the paperwork from the Constellation translated and there is a wealth of information in there. Well done you two." Freddy interrupted "I may be being paranoid Sir George but I felt that we were being followed as we came here today." Sir George replied, "Quite correct young man, you are still being observed by our local Russian friends but how they got onto you so quickly I don't know. Let me tell you one of the main reasons that you were chosen. Pinky here was known to have been the test pilot on the delivery of the first Lockheed Constellation aircraft from the U.S.A. years ago and was therefore most likely competent in all eventualities for the delivery of the Russian missiles on that aircraft. They had to have someone experienced in flying that aircraft as they were stretching the plane to its' limits with the weight that they must have been carrying. It is down to him that you were kidnapped and all traces of your lives erased. Pinky was obviously totally oblivious to that of course and can't take any blame. Had the flight been caught you could tell your captors nothing and so you were not a risk to them. In the event that you succeeded you would be expendable and therefore they could make you disappear without trace. They very nearly succeeded but they did not expect you to survive their trap. I won't ask you how you escaped but it must have been something that only Pinky must have known about. The U.S. authorities could not explain it. They found the wreckage and some of the door remnants and they showed that the doors were very firmly sealed. By the way, the monies that you acquired are being held safely for your future use, it is the least that we can do for you. As you know, it confirms that there has been massive infiltration into all of our departments and armed services. We are in your debt for much of the knowledge that we now have but we still require your help. You are the only people who can recognise some of their agents involved. With your help we can access some of them and make inroads into discovering more of the agents who are working with them. To that end we want you to re-trace your steps from initial kidnap to the flight to Cuba. Will you do that for us?" The boys nodded and Sir George continued, "As you no longer exist you are no longer in the R.A.F. and therefore you will be on our staff until further notice. You will have London accommodation provided and all arrangements made for your general spending and living requirements. A car is waiting for you and one of our most trusted agents who will be working with you. You can leave by a secret exit from here and lose your friends out there. We will do our best to find out how they followed you so quickly. Good luck chaps, all of the other instructions are in the car." They were taken straight away to their new houses, avoiding any possibility of their being followed. They were extremely pleased with their Knightsbridge apartments and spent the morning re-arranging things to their liking. They overlooked Hyde Park barracks and Hyde Park and the rear gardens were very private and not overlooked and the views from the front of the buildings were very pleasing and reassuring. The apartments were in a converted large house which was split into separate dwellings. Just after lunch the agent arrived from the ministry to introduce himself as Charles and he had instructions to take the boys through their recent travels, starting at Marham airbase. Charles presented them with an introductory letter from Sir George to confirm his identity. He was a fresh open faced young man of medium height but seen in public he would not have attracted any specific attention. He appeared very enthusiastic and keen to look after the boys on this mission. He appeared to be in his mid or late twenties and obviously fit and active. He was blond, not very tall and he was casually smartly dressed so that he would not have stood out in a crowd. He explained that he had been in the service now for a few years and had had a rapid move up in rank. Their objective was to learn as much as they could about any of the infiltrators. He described the plan of action by pointing out that the trail started from the boy's journeys to Germany. They would follow that and anywhere it may take them. As they left London Freddy observed the same black car following them again. "Charles, are you aware that we are being followed yet again?" "Yes, they have been with us since we set off." Charles replied. Freddy asked, "Who knew that you were coming for us today?" "As far as I know, only Sir George but he must be working with a small ministry team. It might have got out from there but these agents seem to have had a source within our services for some time. I will let him know that there is a specific leak in one of the departments somewhere tipping off the Russians about your movements. Don't worry we will be losing them in a few minutes, I contacted the office via the car signaller and they should react very soon." They hadn't travelled very far when they saw a police car ahead driving very slowly with a stream of cars behind. People were very reluctant to overtake it and so it was towing a stream of cars. Charles accelerated and overtook the police car but as soon as the following black car overtook, the police car intercepted it bringing them to a halt. That was the last that they saw of the black car and its' occupants. Charles drove in to Upper Marham and then Burnthouse Drove Road. They soon stopped outside of the manor house near Lady's Wood. The manor gates were closed but they opened as

Freddy applied gentle pressure. Memories of their previous visit flooded back and they had a feeling of trepidation as the trio entered the large quadrangle but the place looked deserted and quite strange but how they were not sure. Things had not been disturbed but it looked strangely different and neglected. They quickly checked the areas familiar to them but there was nothing to be found. They stood in the kitchen at a loss and wondering what to do when they heard a muffled sound. No one was sure what it was or where it had originated but as Freddy opened the utility cupboard door they heard it again but louder. In the corner of the cupboard half hidden by the washing machine was Tom. He was trying to hide but the fear that he showed made him shake and groan. "Hello Tom it is only us, there is nothing to be afraid of. Where is Alan?" asked Freddy. Tom hesitated but recognition showed on his face as the fear subsided. "I don't know I only work here. I've always worked here. I thought that they had come back. They threw me out and told me to go away but I sneaked back in and hid here. This is my home. I have nowhere else to go. I heard that Ali man arguing with Alan. There was lots of shouting and then I heard shots being fired. I don't know where Alan is and I haven't seen him since they left. I have nowhere else to go, I have always lived here with Alan I don't know anything other." Tom sounded very shocked and confused. They left Tom for a while in the kitchen having checked that all the food was still there but they soon came back having found no trace of Alan. "So where is everyone Tom?" Pinky asked. "They were all here this morning and then I heard all the shouting. Just after that they all left and I thought it might have been them coming back when I heard you arriving. As they left I heard Ali say something about Whitehall but I don't know of any White Hall near here." "They must be heading for London and if they are going to Whitehall that means that they must have a contact or contacts in the Ministry. Where was the shouting coming from Tom?" Freddy asked. Tom replied "From Alan's office down the corridor there." Tom pointed to the far door in the kitchen. "Come on chaps, we haven't looked down here." Freddy set off through the door and into a long corridor with small rooms to the left and right. When they ate in the kitchen before, Freddy thought that the door leading to this corridor was just a cupboard door and did not realise that there was anything of interest here. Only one room at the end contained anything other than rubbish. This was obviously Alan's office and there was blood all over the floor. The place was full of files and papers but the desk and surrounding area was clear. Charles left them to look for any other signs of violence anywhere in the building. Charles set off through the out buildings looking into all the rooms that had been occupied by staff members at some time. He went into the main building and marvelled at the faded splendour but he found nothing significant. Back outside he headed for the boiler room and as he passed the coal cellar, he spotted the sprawling form of a blood covered body. "That must be Alan." thought Charles. He checked the pockets of the sad figure and found a driving license with a photograph, confirming his fears. Meanwhile Freddy and Pinky searched through the papers in and on Alan's desk. Freddy came across Alan's 'bait tin'. Freddy thought that he had kept his sandwiches in it. That had always puzzled Freddy as the kitchen was always well stocked and Alan didn't seem to go anywhere very often. Why did he need a 'Bait tin'? Freddy was curious and opened the tin to find that if was full of papers and documents. One of the documents was Alan's last will and testament. Freddy glanced through it and found that Alan had left the manor house and a considerable amount of money to Tom. He was the only beneficiary. Freddy had good news for Tom. Charles arrived into Alan's office and told them that he had found the body of a male in his fifties shot through the head and dumped into the coal cellar. It had to be Alan. The trio went back to the kitchen where they found Tom still in a daze. Freddy gently roused Tom and gave him the good news, "You won't need to go anywhere now Tom this is all yours. This is your home." Tom was clutching a photograph and Freddy asked Tom what it was. The question seemed to bring Tom back to reality, "This is Alan and the baby is me. He was like a father to me. When I grew up, I did odd jobs for Alan and got pocket money for looking after the rooms upstairs and any visitors that came. We had lots and lots of people coming here but not as many now. I got a lot of pocket money to look after you." "Look," said Freddy "those awful men won't be coming back and they won't hurt you again. If they had wanted to harm you, they would have done that before they left. We will be sending some men here to look through all of Alan's papers but they are good guys, so don't worry. Is there anyone that we could contact to stay with you for a while?" Tom shook his head. Freddy continued, "We will be leaving very soon but you will be fine and we will come back to see you before too long." They said goodbye to Tom and set off back to London. It seemed that for a change they were not being followed and they returned to London without incident. Although they had assured Tom that he would be alright, none of them was totally convinced about that. Sir George was waiting for them in his office, "I understand that you have found more information for me." Charles reported, "Firstly Sir, we were followed from this office all the way to Marham." "That is impossible," exploded Sir George, "that must mean that there is a leak from this department. Only a handful of people knew of your mission and none of my aids were told. It must have been somebody in the security management team or someone very close to them. I can't believe that someone on my committee has been compromised." "It is the only explanation but I did send you that information by radio earlier today" Charles added. "I agree," said Freddy "we have been followed ever since we got back to 'Blighty'. They knew where we were staying and we were even observed at Petersham Place. Someone very close to you has been supplying the Russian agents with all details of our movements." Charles interrupted "There is a lot of paperwork at the manor house and from what little I read there is some very valuable information in them. I suggest that I take some of the boys in my team to go through it all immediately, not forgetting what the boys told me about Jones in the Customs office. Let the boys lie low for a while Sir." "Good idea," said Sir George "I will be back in touch with you boys when Charles gets all the information back to me and we will take it from there. Your message was not passed on to me so I will check on that. Use only the red priority communications Charles and nobody but you and I will know the content of what you find." The trio left the office and Charles dropped the boys and the car off at Kings Cross

Station and they all took the underground moving from train to train at the last minute to avoid any chance of anyone being able to follow them. They finally left the underground at Battersea station and the boys followed Charles who moved at pace. They went into a car salesroom building and Charles acknowledged the man in the sales office. They left the building by a rear door. Out from the back door they turned right into an alleyway and at the far end they came to a lockup garage which Charles opened and they went in to find a windowless van. Charles drove the van out of the garage with the boys out of sight in the back. They travelled for about fifteen minutes and came to a stop. The van doors opened and the boys found themselves inside of a very large warehouse. They followed Charles up some stairs to an upper floor where Charles opened a door to reveal a spacious, fully furnished apartment. The door leading into the flat was a heavily barred metal door with a spy hole at head height. "This is your temporary home and you will find everything you need in here, follow me. I spent some time here and though it is a back water warehouse there are plenty of things to do" The Boys, followed Charles into one of many side rooms as Charles explained that this was a high security safe house. "In this room there is every sort of disguise that you can imagine in a kit and as you are free to come and go, as you please, make sure that you are not recognized. Try out the disguises they are very good. If you need to contact me, just use the radio here. It is a single frequency unit outside of all public wave bands and untraceable."

    Charles left the boys, promising that he or a trusted agent would check on them at eight-o-clock every morning. He asked them to be sure that no one was allowed to know that they were staying here. He would do his best to keep their whereabouts safe. After a good night's sleep, the boys explored the apartment and the many side rooms. They played around and had great fun with many of the disguises. The day seemed to pass very quickly and they were not concerned that Charles had not visited them this morning. After all he had only left them late last night. They settled down to a relaxing drink in the evening to watch the television but there was the usual rubbish on TV so they chatted and reviewed the recent happenings. The drink flowed and they became rather morose as bed time approached. Charles arrived promptly at eight-o-clock the next morning to make sure that all was well. Charles was correct when he said that there was everything they needed in their 'Suite' as the boys called it. There were clothes, food, drink, money and lots of entertainment. There were six large bedrooms each with shower and toilet. Charles stayed for a while and told them what had been found at the manor but after he had left them, they had a great time trying out some more of the disguises, whiskers, hair pieces and amongst the many clothing outfits, tramps clothing and lots of pieces of string. As they experimented in front of the bathroom mirror with different characters, laughing at the incredible changes, Pinky noticed a lever next to the toilet and traced the attached wire to a catch above the large bathroom window. "Hey have you seen this," said Pinky "this is where they must have brought in all the large pieces of furniture. If we pull this lever the whole window will come out." They opened a small window within the large window to reveal a pulley operated platform that could be controlled by the person on the platform. "Cool." Freddy quipped. They had lunch and then listened to the radio. The news was dominated by the Cuban crisis, relations between the Americans and the Russians had deteriorated. The boys felt some guilt and responsibility for the situation but tried some distraction, playing a game of cards. The evening seemed to drag on and on until they went to their beds.

Charles called the next morning right on time with news of some progress from Sir George. The paperwork from the manor house had given clues to many of the junior infiltrators who were now all under investigation by security services. Charles left them after a while and as he closed and locked the door Freddy said, "Let's try out some of these disguises and get out of here for a while. What about this evening going to a local pub and having drink and a pub meal?" "Yes," replied Pinky "I'd love a change of scenery with a large ice cold gin and tonic.

That is one thing lacking in this place, ice." They played around with more disguises and had a good laugh at some of the characters that they created. One that stood out as a 'must try' were a couple of post men's outfits. They put on wigs, whiskers and eyebrow extensions and when they looked in the bathroom mirror at their reflections, they both agreed that they both looked the part. They left in disguise mid evening as it was getting dark. They walked to the end of the road and there were pubs left and right. The one on the left seemed quieter so they headed for that one, In the King's Head they spent a very pleasant evening playing darts and dominoes with the locals who seemed to accept them for who they were supposed to be without question, two postmen. They got back to the warehouse suite without incident and they were quite excited that they had fitted in to the pub crowd as two postmen. They could not wait to tell Charles all about it in the morning. The boys were up and dressed by seven-o-clock the next morning and they had just cleared away breakfast when the doorbell rang. It wasn't the usual signal so Freddy checked who it was at the door through the spy hole. Charles was standing there with the strangest look of surprise on his face. Freddy unlocked and opened the door but as he did, Charles fell forward into Freddy's arms and as Freddy caught him the thugs burst past him into the suite. Charles was dead and Freddy lowered his body to the floor. Charles still had that innocent surprised look on his face, like a child full of wonderment, questioning what he saw. They had been taken completely by surprise by the seven intruders and Ali was amongst them. Freddy recognised him immediately and noticed that he was the only one of them who was not carrying a firearm. Two armed men grabbed hold of Freddy and another two held Pinky. Ali broke the stunned silence, "You have caused us a lot of trouble and cost us a number of our agents. You will tell us what you took from the manor house and what you already know, you will tell us everything." From the way Ali was talking he didn't know anything about the papers on the aircraft. Freddy blurted out, "We only know what you told us, we know nothing more." Ali slapped Freddy across his face, "Liar! You took papers from the house the boy told us." Pinky interjected, "The man who took the papers is the one that you have just murdered." Ali walked slowly over to Pinky and taking a gun out of his associates' jacket, he hit Pinky on the chin with the butt of the handgun causing a gash to open up on the point of his Pinky's chin and he slumped forward unconscious. Blood flowed out of Pinky's chin as he laid on the floor. Pinky groaned as he quickly started to regain his senses. "Look Ali, I'll tell you all I know and this sort of thing is not necessary. Let me take Pinky to the bathroom to clean him up and we will tell you all we know about the things that we have discovered." Ali agreed to let Freddy take Pinky to the bathroom but they were escorted by two of the thugs. The other intruders were sent to look round the suite for any information the boys may have hidden. Ali slumped onto a settee, "Don't be long boys I don't like to be kept waiting." Freddy nearly carried Pinky along the corridor to the bathroom where he sat him on the toilet seat whilst he went to the sink for a face cloth and towel. The two gunmen went to the window to look for any chance of possible escape out of the window. Suddenly there was a great loud crash as the heavy window frame fell from its' mounting crashing down on top of the gunmen. One of the men was dead on impact as the window handle crashed through his chest cavity killing him instantly. The other gunman was rendered completely unconscious. Pinky had timed the pull of the lever next to the toilet to perfection, catching both men totally unaware and leaving them no chance of avoiding the full weight of the metal and glass window. The noise of the crash was partially cushioned by the gunmen and the rest of the gunmen were too far away to hear anything to arouse alarm. Freddy handed the wet cloth to Pinky to wipe the worst of the blood away. On inspection the cut was not as bad as first thought but the flow of blood made it look like a serious injury. Some of the disguises were still in the bag in the bathroom when they had been messing about the previous day. "You grab the make-up tin Pinky and I'll bring the rest of the stuff." Without delay they left the bathroom by the window climbing onto the pulley platform outside. Freddy turned the pulley handle as fast as he could and they reached the ground in seconds. They were at the rear of the warehouse in the loading yard. Freddy remembered the shed that was on a piece of spare ground next to the Kings Head, "Quick this way we'll head for that shed near the Kings Head. Are you alright Pinky?" "I'll make it." He replied. They made it to the shed without any problems. The door was wide open as they reached it and they shut it as soon as they were inside. The smell was awful but, in the circumstances, it was of little consequence. The bleeding had stopped after keeping the pressure of the towel for some time applied to Pinky's chin. His face was a bit of a mess, "You need some whiskers to cover that lot up so let's make up as the tramps and it will not be obvious to anyone looking closely at you that you have had any injury. It is also fitting as tramps in this place, it stinks." They worked on their disguises and with each other's help and lots of string, they really looked the part. When they were fully disguised Pinky sat on an upturned beer crate and Freddy on a pile of sacks in the corner. They planned to wait until dark before they ventured out to allow the Russian group to complete their search. No doubt the Russians were checking everywhere for them by now. The noise of people running and shouting got closer and closer and the boys held their breaths. The door smashed open and a gun waving Ali was framed in the doorway. The speed of the opening door caused an uncontrolled look of surprise on the occupants faces and Ali saw, what appeared to be, two down and out tramps of little consequence. In his fury Ali thought to rid the world of such low life but he realised that the sound of his gun would attract too much attention and his quarry would be lost for good. The boys feared the worst but Ali was hit by the smell and saw two old tramps squatting in a shed, he cursed and left without delay. The unbelieving pair stared at each other in stunned silence. They couldn't believe their good fortune, they had completely fooled Ali and his gang and as the noise faded, they got to their feet and carefully left the shed. They took their disguise kit with them knowing they might really need it again. It took a lot of nerve to slowly shamble down the street away from the warehouse. Every sinew in their body wanted to flee as fast as they could but they maintained their shambling gait all the way to the underground station. They were heading for Sir George and a promise of some security. They were not completely sure that Sir George wasn't the leak but they had to take the chance that he was not the traitor as he was their only contact. At the ministry they had difficulty persuading the guard who they were but as they removed some of the whiskers, he let them pass and they were taken to Sir

George's office. "No one knew where we were, how did the Russian group know? It has to be someone very close to you or the only other explanation is that you are the leak Sir George," accused Freddy and he continued without waiting for a reply "Charles was murdered on the information given by whoever is The infiltrator." He continued and told Sir George the whole story of events at the warehouse. Sir George did not react other than to repeat over and over, "My God!" From Sir George's reactions it was plain to see that he was totally devastated by the story of what had happened to them and in particular the death of Charles. His head swam with the thoughts that began to become clear to him and the implications were unthinkable. Eventually he gathered himself to speak "You boys have been very resourceful and I am so pleased that you are okay after what you have been through. You are absolutely correct to suspect me as we don't know who we can trust. Charles was my nephew and I just don't know how I'm going to break the news to my brother. Would you two like to get out of that gear? You can use my private bathroom through there. Please use any clothing that you find suitable in my word-robe. The boys returned later smelling a lot sweeter and looking more like themselves but events had left marks on them both. Sir George was pouring a large whisky as the boys came back, "I am sure that you could do with a snifter as much as me." He poured two more large whiskies and continued "you took the right action and I am proud that you had the gumption to doubt me as well but you can be assured that we are reading from the same song sheet. You are right that it must be someone very close to me who is the traitor. We took every precaution to make sure that no one outside of our meetings could possibly overhear or record our planning. You chaps must have someone in mind seeing as you took the risk of coming back here?" He drained his glass and looked unblinking at the boys. Freddy answered "We went through all of the committee members but there was no one who could possibly know of all of our movements the one common factor is Petersham Place. No one knew that we were there at the beginning but we were followed as soon as we left the house. How did they know when no one on our side knew? When Charles picked us up to go to Marham we were followed from the off. Who knew? To check on any of our suspicions we need to set a trap. Whoever it responsible is masterminding their operations from this district." They decided to leave the final planning until the morning and Sir George offered them overnight accommodation in his office suite guest rooms. As they prepared to retire for the night the telephone rang and a voice at the other end told Sir George that Godfrey Bellinger was here to see him. Sir George agreed to see him and after a few minutes there was a knock at the door. "Come in Godfrey." said Sir George and as Godfrey came into the room, he was startled to see the boys sitting there. "What is it Godfrey?" asked Sir George. It took Godfrey a few seconds to recover from his shock, "I came to tell you that young Cubby is trying to contact Freddy and Pinky about a re-union and I was going to ask you to pass on the message when you saw them again. I thought it better to deliver the message in person rather than risk a phone call." Sir George was thoughtful and finally said "Tell Cubby to call at my office first thing in the morning and I will make arrangements for them to meet up. Thank you, Godfrey." It was the signal for Godfrey to leave so he bade them goodnight and left the office. The interruption awakened them all and they decided to have another night cap. As they sipped their whiskies Sir George said "I have been thinking and I have my doubts about Sir Aubrey Witheringshaw. If I let him and only him know about tomorrow's meeting with Cubby then if things go wrong, we have our culprit." "Well, you may be right Sir but we also know that Godfrey knows, why not just leave it at that and at least clear Godfrey. Involving someone else now may cloud the issue." "You are right Freddy as things stand it will be clear cut. Well chaps let's call it a night." They set off for a much-needed night's sleep. The guest rooms were superior to any hotel that the boys had experienced and the fridge was fully stocked and lacked any price tags. The next morning Cubby arrived at the ministry quite early and was shown in to see Sir George. The boys were in the next office waiting for the signal to go in to meet Cubby. "Good morning, Cubby, do sit down. Now tell me about this re-union that you want to arrange." Sir George sat down behind his desk. Cubby told the story of the crew and their regular meetings and how they planned if and when they were separated to keep up the tradition of getting back together on a regular basis. Godfrey had told Cubby that the boys were back and in London and the crew had come to London to meet up with them and get the story of recent events. "Well," said Sir George and the boys came in at the signal "you had better talk to them yourself." The boys greeted Cubby and said that they would like to get back with the crew and as agreed with Sir George they would meet that afternoon at the 2i's Coffee Bar in Wardour Street. Cubby was delighted to see the boys in good spirits and questioned if it was a good idea for them to meet after hearing a little about recent events. He was assured that it fitted their plans exactly. They chatted for a short time and Sir George broke up the meeting so that he could talk to the boys. Cubby left and Sir George then said "We will be in force looking out for you this afternoon in the event that an attempt is made on you at the Coffee Bar. The waiting about was the worst but at the appointed time the boys arrived in Wardour Street and went downstairs in the 2i's. The crew was already there and a rowdy cheer went up at the sight of the boys coming down to the cellar. "At least we are too early for the music," said Pinky "so we can have a good old chat." The meeting went on for a good two hours and they were all full of coffee by the time they parted with promise of another get together soon. The crew had been partially included in the past events but they had only a very limited knowledge of the implications. The boys left Wardour Street and headed for

Picadilly Circus and then on to the ministry. They had not seen any of the backup promised by Sir George but no doubt it was there somewhere. Back in Sir George's office Sir George said "I am pleased to report that there were no incidents or sightings anywhere during your meeting so that rules out Godfrey." The phone rang and it was Godfrey "I have Cubby here for you Sir George." "Hello Sir. Godfrey was saying that he thought it might be alright for Freddy and Pinky to come to Petersham Place this evening. The crew and I have decided to have a quiet drink together and they may be staying over for the night?" "Well, I can't see any problem with that, just hold," and he asked the boys if they were agreed "yes that seems to be in order they will be on their way shortly." Sir George put the phone down. "I will send an escort with you at a discreet distance just in case and we will keep a watch if you chose to stay overnight. Have fun boys." They left and headed to Petersham Place in a ministry car followed at a distance by the escort car. They arrived at Godfrey's to be greeted by Cubby and Godfrey on the doorstep. There was a lot of back slapping and cheery greetings when they met the crew again and the questions came fast and furious from the crew members. The boys could not answer some of the queries as they were security sensitive. Godfrey had gone to another part of the building to allow the chaps to chat and reminisce and it was all alien talk to him anyway he had said. The boys had a final drink before leaving and they were preparing to go when the front door smashed open sending splintering wood flying all around. Ali and a group of armed men burst into the house and a volley of gun fire was heard throughout the house. Freddy and Pinky hit the ground at the same time and each wondered if the other had been shot. Shots continued to ring out and the boys lay on the ground for what seems like an age until silence took over, Freddy raised his head and gave an audible gasp. The room and entrance passage were quiet and Freddy could the dead forms of Ali and his gang on the floor. Sir George stood in the doorway and shouted "Is everybody ok?" The crew gradually got to their feet stunned by what had just happened and the reply came from weak voices "We think so." Sir George asked "Is that the famous Ali?" Ali was laid on the floor in a most unnatural position, "Yes that's him," replied Freddy. "Right let's get you all out of here," said Sir George and turned to leave but suddenly stopped "Where is Godfrey?" No one had seen him during all the noise and confusion so a search was made by the security men and he was discovered unconscious on the upstairs landing. Sir George roused him and made sure that he was alright before he left for the ministry with the boys. At the ministry Sir Aubrey was being held in the interrogation room. He had been informed about the 2i's meeting and even though nothing had happened there he was being questioned anyway. The security team had worked on him all night but Sir Aubrey maintained that he had not divulged the information to anyone. Eventually he was released under house arrest. The boys remained at the ministry building but they did not see any of the security service team including Sir George. The boys felt as if they were under house arrest as they were not allowed out of the building for their own safety. Later that evening there was a knock on their door. The door opened and Sir George entered "Well chaps, we have been all day checking on Sir Aubrey's movements and contacts and we have drawn a total blank. It seems to be as he told us because it seems impossible for him to have been in touch with anyone. All his calls and activities have been monitored from the time I told him to the time we arrested him. I think that you and I will have to go and have another chat to him." The boys set off with Sir George, pleased at last to get out of the ministry building. They were driven under escort to Sir Aubrey's house in Knightsbridge. As they approached his house there was something very wrong. There were security cars in numbers outside of his house and the door was wide open. Sir George leapt from the car as it came to a halt with the boys in pursuit. They went in through the open door and were taken upstairs by one of the security agents to Sir Aubrey's bed room. There on the bed lay Sir Aubrey who was clearly dead with half of his head blown away by gunshot. He was still grasping a heavy gage weapon in his right hand still pointing to the side of his head that had been blown away. "Well chaps, I don't know how he did it but it looks like a clear-cut expression of guilt. He must have known that we were on to him and he committed suicide." Sir George concluded. He turned to leave and then stopped in his tracks "That's all wrong," he said "he was left-handed and a bullet of that Caliber would be small entry and large exit site. His right index finger is on the trigger and he suffered from Dupuytren's syndrome in his right hand the index finger on the trigger was totally rigid and could not possibly have fired the gun. This is a murder case. Search the room for any clues that could tell us who else was here. Come on chaps let's leave them to get on with it." They left the building and set off back to the ministry with their escort. Back in the office Sir George reviewed the situation "This puts a totally different complexion on this. Sir Aubrey was completely innocent but someone wanted us to think otherwise. How did this get out when no one else knew about it?" They sat a while thinking things through when Freddy suddenly said "I have been thinking about all of the incidents involving pursuers since we arrived back in England and I hope that you chaps can prove me wrong. The only person who has been the common factor in all of this is Cubby's cousin Godfrey Bellinger. I know that we found him unconscious at his house but was he genuine or was it purely for us to see? Was he just putting it on? We didn't see any injury on him." Sir George and Pinky stared at him. After some thought Sir George said "You may have a point Freddy but I hope that you are wrong, even so we cannot discount or disprove what you say so we will have to change our thinking and adopt a different emphasis." Sir George picked up the phone to call Godfrey "Hello Godfrey, how are you? Great so can you come around to my office in the morning to discuss some new information that we have discovered. First thing will be fine." The following morning, they boys were in Sir George's office early waiting for Godfrey to arrive when an agent involved in yesterday evening's events knocked on the office door. Sorry to bother you sir but we got a call from Godfrey Bellinger a few minutes ago asking about Sir Aubrey Witheringshaw and the chap who answered told him that he had been murdered. We called at his house to bring him here as arranged but the house was deserted and much of Bellinger's personal belongings were missing." "Thank you, agent Blaze you can stand down," Sir George waved his hand dismissing the agent and continued "It looks as if you were correct Freddy we have our leak." He picked up the phone and asked records to do a full check on the background of Godfrey Bellinger without delay. Fifteen minutes later a secretary handed a file to Sir George. He sat reading it intently for a while and suddenly he thumped the desk "I'll have someone's head for this, incompetence, absolute bloody incompetence. Godfrey worked with John Cairncross in the ministry of supply in fifty-seven. Cairncross worked with Kim Philby and they are both suspected double agents and under ongoing investigation. This should have been picked up years ago. We have to find Godfrey without delay it looks like we have found the hub of the infiltration of Russian agents. We are investigating the content of messages sent by within the coding used. All the messages were sent through Berlin where your friend Ali was based. This is Cairncross and Philby and while nothing seems amiss with the content security have uncovered possible code just one big mess and we would not have the leads that we have now if it had not been for you boys. You have opened a 'Pandoras box' giving us a massive job ahead to identify these traitors. That fool of an agent who informed Bellinger of our knowledge of the murder alerted him to the fact that we weren't fooled by their set up. He knew straight away that we would suspect him now that Sir Aubrey was known to be an innocent victim. You chaps have been invaluable in this matter and I hope that you are going to see this thing through? In fact, I hope that you will be happy to come onto our staff being fully employed in security." Freddy and Pinky looked at each other and nodded their agreement. "Thank Sir." They both said. "Well done chaps welcome aboard. Now you two must lay low and out of circulation for a while until we make sure that you are no longer prime targets. The next day the boys sat in the ministry building apartment "We can't just sit around here all the time," said Freddy "let's get out before I lose my sanity. We can get out disguise kit out and see what we can do." They both agreed and played around with different disguise characters applying false noses, moustaches and eyebrows. With clear glass spectacles they effected a complete transformation. They spend the rest of the day walking around and exploring London town. They were acutely aware that they may be being followed so they took a variety of evasive actions but they saw nothing suspicious and were sure that they were alone. They got back to the ministry late evening and entered using the passes arranged before they left. The guard was very suspicious as he did not recognise them but the passes were effective. They had just removed their disguises when Sir George entered. "Hello chaps. Godfrey has flown the coop. He left early this morning as we were learning that he was no longer at his home. He left by plane from London City Airport and we have a team there looking for any information that might lead us to his whereabouts. His flight was tracked to Berlin but he appears to have parachuted just before they made Berlin airspace. We must go and find him." "We were roped into this at the beginning by Carl," said Freddy "he worked in the mess at our Berlin supply base he must have had contact with their operation in Germany. He may not know about events here in the U.K. so he may not know what our involvement is now. If we talk to him then we might get some good leads as to where Godfrey might be." "Good plan," said Sir George "we'll set off first thing tomorrow. I will arrange the flight tonight and we will get to Germany before lunch time. Leave it all to me. My aide will give you a morning call." Sir George left them and they looked at each other with the joint feeling of 'here we go again.' Early the next morning they set off in a private jet to Germany. They had driven straight onto the air strip and boarded straight from the car. They were both thankful that there wasn't a long car journey to the airport this time. They landed at the air force base and went straight to the mess. They asked for Carl but they were told that he hadn't been seen for a week failing to do his shifts and being threatened with dismissal when he did show up. They asked where they could find him and reluctantly the mess manager gave them the last known address for Carl. Sir George made a quick telephone call from the mess and as they left a car pulled up at the door followed by two escort vehicles. They got into the leading car and headed for Carl's last known address which was a farm only ten minutes from the air base. The driver was local and knew the farm well. The farm looked as if it had not been tended for years and the outbuildings were in a very run down state. As they drew up to the farmhouse, they could see that the farm door was wide open and as they went in it was clear that the farm had not been occupied for days. "Check all the rooms and outhouses for anything that could help us locate Carl." Sir George ordered. Freddy checked the fire place to see if there was any warmth in the hearth. As he knelt down to feel the coals in the grate, he could see the soot covered back plate on the chimney. The fire was cold but as he looked closer Freddy could see written in the soot 'Zeestow Kirche'. "Have a look at this Sir George it means nothing to me but maybe it is what we are looking for." Sir George bent down to look 'Zeestow Kirche'." he said. "What was that Sir?" said one of the escorts and Sir George repeated "'Zeestow Kirche'." "I know it well Sir," said the agent "it is not far from Berlin near Wustermark." "Ok, let's go." said Sir George and he made for the door. The convoy headed for Berlin and had only been travelling for a few minutes when four motor cycles caught up with them and drew alongside the boy's car. The bikers opened fire with handguns but as the car was bullet proof they came to no harm as the doors and windows were sprayed with bullets. The two escort cars immediately returned fire and three of the bikers died before they hit and bounced along the road. The fourth and last biker wobbled along the road for some was before going off the road and crashing into the trees lining the road. The rear escort car stopped and two agents went to see where the biker was. They found him barely conscious but obviously dying. They asked him in German who had sent him and he barked a venomous response which proved to be too much effort and his spirit departed from his mortal remains. "Did he say anything?" Sir George asked. "Nothing sir just a nasty curse in Russian." Sir George made a quick phone call and they all got back to their vehicles and continued on their way. Freddy enquired about the phone call and Sir George informed them that he had contacted the 'Tidy Team'. "They will make sure that the dead attackers will be taken before anyone spots them and makes a nuisance of themselves." They arrived at the church in Zeestow as the light was fading. The armed escort entered the church first but the building was empty. The church and the back rooms offered no clues as to the whereabouts of Carl. "Where do we go from here?" Freddy asked Sir George. He ordered another search of the interior and exterior of the building but no matter how hard they tried they couldn't find a thing. The place was clean, possibly too clean. Someone had used the building but then had it very professionally cleaned. No finger prints on anything, no litter, nothing. They decided to leave and move on to Berlin in the hope of finding some clues there. Freddy was last to leave but as he was closing the door he heard 'tip, tip, tip', 'tap, tap, tap' 'tip, tip, tip' it was the sound of metal on metal. He called to Sir George and when he arrived back, he told him to listen. Freddy said "It is Morse code Sir S.O.S." "By God you're right" he replied "Get everyone back I want that noise traced now." Freddy went to the nearest radiator and tapped loudly. The response was immediate. "There's someone wherever the boiler is located Sir." The order was given to find a cellar or boiler room quickly. It took a while for one of the agents to find a stone trap door in the vestry. The trap door was a heavy concrete slab and took two people to lift it. Stone steps led down below the church itself. Agents with torches ventured down the stone steps to a dark cellar below and found Carl, his wife and two children chained to the heating pipes. Carl had been tapping his chains on the pipe in the hope that someone would hear his S.O.S. He had been tapping constantly for days not knowing if it was day or night down in the depths of the church. He was very weak and his family was in a very distressed condition and were in need of urgent medical help. Freddy found a light switch and luckily there was still an electricity supply. The cellar burst into bright light. Carl recognised Pinky and Freddy immediately "I thought that they had killed you both. Thank God they didn't and you came after me. My family and I owe our lives." Freddy asked him "Who brought you here?" "They brought us here just after you picked up your last load of cigarettes and whisky. You had just left when a gang of Russian speaking gunmen forced me into a car. They took me to the farm and picked up Helga and the children. I overheard them mention Zeestow and the church and left a message for anyone to find. They brought us straight here and we've been here until you arrived a few minutes ago. Some hours ago, now they came back and one of the Russians came back to kill us but an English man told him to put his gun away. He did not want anyone to know that they were here and the noise might attract attention."

Freddy continued "Did you know the English man?" "No but I heard them talking about getting to East Berlin and one of the Russians called him Billinner." "Could it have been Bellinger?" asked Freddy. Carl smiled and nodded. The escort agents got them released from their chains and made arrangements for them to be taken to hospital for a checkup and then home. Carl's involvement was not a matter for British Security. They left Carl and his family with lots of hugs and kisses from the girls and as they travelled on to Berlin Sir George updated them. "You two still have no identities you still don't exist so we have to do something about that without delay. I propose to give you fresh identities with bank accounts and everything you need to provide a history for yourselves. Our northern agent has stood down in retirement now after his last mission to find you both. His imaginary identity is now vacant but the name carries history and essentials. You can become the brothers Huntley G. Haverstock and Huntley J. Haverstock." Pinky interrupted "Thank you sir but after this is all over, I propose to retire as well. I was thinking of retiring from the R.A.F. before all of this and after all that has happened, I am more than sure now." "Well, if you are sure Pinky, "said Sir George "you know that the rewards are very good and with benefits but if I can't change your mind?" "No," replied Pinky "I think that I could do with putting my feet up from now on." "In that case we will make sure that your future needs in retirement are taken care of." As Sir George continued talking to Freddy, Pinky cast his mind back to the time in married quarters and his life with Mary. Soon after the war finished Pinky met his childhood sweetheart and they soon wed. They got accommodation in married quarters and they tried for a family but their efforts were not productive. His brother had three children and the Air force life meant that contact with family was very unusual. His wife Mary died after a severe stroke and his loss made him yearn for family. This was his chance to contact what family he had left and he was determined to take this chance to retire. He was soon to be retired from the R.A.F. anyway and this was the sooner prospect. Freddy was quite happy to continue the tradition as Huntley G. Haverstock and though Sir George was prepared to drop the G. which was no longer required for identification, Freddy was quite happy with it. Sir George said that all would be in place before they got back to England. As they entered West Berlin their car was stopped by a sergeant M.P. "Sir

George?" he enquired. Sir George nodded. "We have a message for you from a double agent in East Berlin. It makes no sense to us but I am sure that it is important sir. Agent Stiller wants to defect to the West and he has sent this note to aid his cause." He handed the note to Sir George and he read it very carefully, "Thank you sergeant that is all. This is an old code but it appears that Godfrey has been in touch with the Eastern Block agency and is looking for their help to cross over immediately from West Berlin to East Berlin. He has given his position at a known safe house in Friedrich Strasse near the station. Driver, if you know this place, then let's go. We don't want him getting across the wall." The driver knew the place well as it was near a regular exchange point at the bridge in Friedrich Strasse. As they headed there, they were joined by two more escort cars filled with armed agents. Friedrich Strasse was still showing the damage from the allied bombing of World War II. They arrived at a bomb site rubble strewn area close to the safe house and the place was surrounded before Sir George and the occupants of the new cars went in unannounced. They were not challenged or impeded by the Russian agents who were inside. They all had legitimate reasons for being there, sanctioned by the West Berlin authorities. There was no sign of Bellinger. The Russian agents gave them no sensible answers to their questions and they gave no indication that they knew what Sir George was talking about. Sir George respected the training that these agents had undergone and he knew that any further interrogation at this time would not help their immediate need to find the whereabouts of Godfrey. Suddenly Freddy saw Bellinger out of the rear window running across the open ground at the back of the house. Two of Sir George's men appeared and Bellinger opened fire on the one nearer to him hitting the agent in the thigh. As the agent fell to the ground Bellinger ran into a hail of bullets, killing him instantly. Sir

George was furious he wanted Bellinger alive "Take this lot and incarcerate them." The Russian agents were led away and they made no fuss as they knew that they would not be held for long. Sir George turned and left the building knowing that they could do no more in Berlin. Before they reached the car the Sergeant M.P. handed another note to Sir George from Stiller. He thanked his German escort team for all of their help and the trio was taken to the nearest airfield where they took off for home. They were all disappointed that Bellinger had died in the exchange as he had information that would have expedited their search for the other agents. Not much was said but Sir George appeared to sit the whole journey fuming and muttering to himself. The boys had never seen him behave in such a way and they were very concerned to see him like this. When they got back Freddy and Pinky moved into two pleasant and spacious furnished apartments above an Italian restaurant on Victoria Embankment yards away from the Houses of Parliament. Whitehall was just around the corner. There was talk that the Government had future plans to take the whole block over but nothing had ever happened. It was a pleasant change to be away from the ministry and the feeling of freedom was a tonic. The next few days turned into weeks of pleasant freedom and fun. Soho and all the mysteries of the area became second nature to them. They had a more relaxing time in the 2i's than they had the first time that they had been there. They regularly visited it and listened to the well-known singers and performers that appeared nightly in the music bar such as Vince Eager and the Vagabonds, Wee Willie

Harris, Ricky Towns and a new duo from Newcastle called Nivram, later to become known as the Shadows. They enjoyed the shows that appeared in the many of the theatres in the district. Life was good. They had plenty of money and they enjoyed each other's company. The memories of Germany etc. were, beginning to fade and after a relaxing evening in town they were preparing to retire for the night when there was a knock at Freddy's door. Freddy opened the door to see Sir George standing there "Come in Sir." Freddy said. "Sorry to call at such a late hour but I needed you to be put in the picture. You will remember as we left Berlin we received a communication from Stiller in East Berlin. It contained a message within the message. I have the results of the de-coding. It seems that Bellinger was the deputy director of operations in England and in charge of a large number of Russian agents many of whom we have now arrested. It means that the director is still operating. That means that you two are still at risk. They still need to know what information you have and what you took in the paperwork that you found. The people who could tell them are now dead or in custody. That leaves you two. We are investigating a number of known agents including Godfrey's pals Kim Philby and John Cairncross. We have some leads to some undersecretaries but we have no concrete evidence to back up our suspicions. That brings me to why I am here." Freddy was ahead of him in thinking that they were to be the carrots to be dangled as Sir George continued "We need your help to flush out whoever is the director. Our two main suspects are two undersecretaries and I am sending some selective information to them. One will be given correct information and one will receive a distraction. With your agreement I am going to tell them both that you have some Russian papers not yet disclosed to us, some that you collected from the Cuban flight. It may of course be a little dangerous so I am asking you before I set things in motion and give out the information. Their agents have been very quiet since Bellinger died but we have news of some great event being planned by them and it is imminent. We have to take action very quickly." Freddy gave his reassurance "You can rely on me Sir." "Good man, get a good night's sleep and I will see you at my office in the morning at nine-o-clock." Freddy arrived in good time at the ministry office and was shown straight in. "Good morning, Huntley do come in. Let me introduce you to Sir James Robert undersecretary from the ministry." Freddy shook hands. "I have been discussing with Sir James about these papers of yours. Do tell how you came to have these papers with information on Russian agents in the U.K." Sir George was relying on Freddy's ingenuity and discretion to play the charade with Sir James. Freddy duly went through the story of their escape from the Cuban air flight and how they found a lot of papers all in Russian. He failed to give the actual details of their method of escape and he wasn't sure why he kept that information from him. He told Sir James that he still had some of the papers that contained names and information that he had not yet handed over to Sir George as they were still being translated. Freddy finished by saying "If you want, I can get them to you sometime tomorrow, Sir George." "That would be fine Huntley," agreed Sir George "how do intend to get them to me?" "I can bring them to your office in the morning." Sir George turned to Sir James "That seems to be a good idea. Well let's go to your club Sir James for an early brunch. That will be all Huntley, until tomorrow." He was leading Freddy by the arm to the office door and once out of earshot of Sir James he said "Well done Freddy I'll be in touch later today at your apartment if that is ok?" "I'll look forward to it Sir." Freddy left the ministry and set off back to the Italian restaurant below his apartment for a welcome cup of Italian coffee. Mario was one of the younger boys at the restaurant and his duties were to invite and greet people outside. Mario saw Freddy returning and greeted him warmly, showing him to a table in the window. Freddy sat with his coffee overlooking the Thames and watching the boats on the river and the people pass by. He thought about the challenges ahead and hoped that Sir George had reliable security people capable of keeping him safe. Sir George had been true to his word and set up a Huntley

Haverstock bank account, credit cards and ministry top priority passes. On checking his new account, it contained more money than he had ever dreamed of. He and Pinky had lunch in the downstairs restaurant and Pinky set off for the city. Freddy went up to his apartment and saw ahead of him Sir George making his way up the stairs. They went into the apartment together. "Well done this morning you handled it very well. If Sir James is our man, then I don't think that he suspected a thing and swallowed your story hook, line and sinker. You are now in great danger if that is the case and Sir James contacts his Russian agents. You need to be armed and we will protect you as well as we can. You have had weapons training I assume during your training so a hand gun will not be new to you. I am taking you to the boffins to familiarise you with some gadgets and a new bullet proof car. You'll like this sporty new model, let's go." Sir George's car was outside waiting and they set off for the Boffin's secret building near Whitehall. They turned into a private garage entry that opened up to reveal a covered interior quadrangle packed with cars and other vehicles. They went upstairs to an office and Freddy was introduced to Rupert who was in charge of field weapons development. Rupert was a dour character who was fully absorbed in his work which left a lot to be desired on the subject of people skills. On introduction Rupert walked to the office door without acknowledging Freddy in any way. Rupert led them both to a very large upstairs workshop and spent most of the afternoon explaining in detail a variety of gadgets and the special features of his new bullet proof sports car. When Freddy drove up to the Italian restaurant following the ordeal that had been time with Rupert there was a parked car outside waiting for his return. The waiting car driver got out of his car and came over to Freddy "Huntley Haverstock?" Freddy nodded. "We are to take you to see the Home Secretary. Here is my I.D. You can follow us in your car if you wish." "I'll do that." Freddy replied. He was conscious that they may not be what they claimed to be. The cars were parked and he was actually taken to see the Home Secretary. "Huntley Haverstock?" the Home Secretary enquired. "Yes Sir." "I understand that you have now joined the service from the R.A.F. and you have already been on mission to Berlin?" "Yes sir." Freddy agreed. "What was all that about lad?" Freddy thought that that was a strange question to come from a Home

Secretary. He also did not like the way that he was being questioned. Something was not as it should be here. Freddy answered "We were following a Russian double agent Godfrey Bellinger." "Are yes and he escaped into East Berlin no doubt?" He looked as if he did not know about the outcome in Berlin. "No sir he was shot and killed by a German security officer in a shootout." The Home Secretary was visibly shocked and then very angry. "Welcome to the service. That will be all." He turned and left the office leaving Freddy to find his own way out. Freddy got back to his car and drove the few blocks along Whitehall to Sir George's ministry office. Freddy explained to him the events of the visit to the Home Secretary but he didn't say anything about his personal impressions. "I do believe that the Home Secretary knew nothing about what happened in Berlin." Freddy said. "No, I told no one hoping that someone would let us know that they knew. However, the Russian agents being held in Berlin have been in custody longer than we expected and so the other side will not have been told. "Thank you for letting me in on this I'm sure that the Home Secretary will be on my back complaining about not being told. I'll tell him that the memo sent from Berlin at the time must have gone astray, mislaid or misdirected or something such. I'll be in touch with you in the morning." Freddy and Pinky spent the evening in town and Pinky told Freddy about the arrangements that had been made for him to retire back in his home town. Pinky would be leaving early in the morning and so they had a farewell drink together tonight. Freddy was sorry that Pinky did not want to stay in London but he did have family back home and as far as he knew they must think that he was dead. It wasn't fair to let them continue with that thought. They spent their final evening together discussing events and reminiscing about their R.A.F. lives together. They did not stay out too late and they had a final meal together in the Italian restaurant. The restaurant owners were also sorry to hear that Pinky was leaving. The following morning before going to see Sir George they said their goodbyes and Pinky headed for his home town. Freddy went to deliver the non-existent papers to Sir George and the whole thing went off without incident. "Well, that clears those two chaps. Nothing happened with either of the set ups. If the opposition knew what had been discussed they would have moved heaven and earth to stop you passing such delicate information to me. We are back to square one Huntley." "Maybe not sir." said Freddy and he related his feelings and impressions with regard to the meeting of the Home Secretary. "You cannot be serious. We can't start an investigation into the affairs of the Home-Secretary, the press would be on it like a rocket and it would be public knowledge within hours. It would cause such serious repercussions that we could not risk it even if you are right." Sir George exclaimed. "We could set the same trap for him that we set for the other two. News of that will not be general knowledge. We could send him a memo telling him that I will be delivering the papers to you in a couple of hours' time. We have nothing to lose and it would at the least satisfy my suspicions." "I don't know if we could get away with it but as you say at this stage what have we to lose. Too much is at stake and time is short. Thinking about it, he is informed of all operations, well nearly all of them. He does have the knowledge and the opportunity to disclose information. Very well I'll send it right away by hand with time set at mid-day." Freddy left the office and spent the next hour and a half considering what could and might happen. He hoped that Sir George had sufficient resources to deal with any trouble that could occur. As the appointed time aproached he went to his car and set off to meet Sir George. He noticed a car set off behind him driving in the same direction. He turned past the Houses of Parliament and into Whitehall. The car followed and as he prepared to turn into the security building car park a car intercepted him and stopped directly in front of him. The following car stopped behind him blocking any attempt to escape in his car. The front car's doors were flung open and four men aimed their firearms directly at Freddy. Freddy froze as he sat trapped in his car. Suddenly, as if from nowhere, armed men surrounded the three cars and their occupants. Warning shots were fired and the raiders dropped their weapons and were taken into custody. People passing by thought that it must be a film set and applauded as the men were taken into custody and looked around wondering if they were themselves on camera. Freddy got out of his car and Sir George walked towards him. "You, okay?" he asked and Freddy nodded "It looks as if you were right after all. The only thing now to do is to confront the Home Secretary but it is a delicate situation. We could have a national crisis on our hands." Freddy replied "We have no choice sir, he is a liability and still dangerous and as soon as he finds out what happened here you could be next on his hit list." "We will go alone you and I, that way we will not attract any unwanted attention." Sir George concluded. They walked together along Whitehall and straight up to the Home Secretary's office. As they went, they brushed aside all challenges and walked unannounced into the Home Secretary's room. "What is the meaning of this Curswell?" The two men in his office were told by Sir George to wait outside. The Home Secretary who had put all attention onto Sir George suddenly realised that Freddy was behind him and the shock registered on his face. "Yes, sir it is Huntley Haverstock and he is alive and well. No doubt you did not expect to ever see him again. "Er, yes I met him here this morning to welcome him to the service." Sir George interrupted him "Yes and then you ordered him to be taken by your friends. They are now in custody and singing like song birds." "What nonsense is this?" he blustered but it showed on his face that he wasn't so confident. Sir George continued "You know full well what this is about. You have led a group of Russian agents who have been infiltrated into the senior positions in many of Her Majesties administrative services. Many of these infiltrators have been identified and dealt with, some severely. You will announce that you are taking a short break and come with us." Sir George picked up the phone and ordered a car. "You have no proof and you can't get away with this." The Home Secretary objected but not very convincingly. "You will find that we can do and have done. We do have proof and we will collect further proof very soon. You are under arrest and you will be taken into custody. Special service agents had been called and they led him from his office and the two men found in his office were also taken for questioning. The Prime Minister was informed of events and he gave instructions on the best way to deal with a very delicate situation. The media must not be allowed to get hold of any knowledge of it. All must be "hush hush", he told Sir George. The offices and London home of the Home Secretary were searched for evidence but it was only when his country residence was searched, did they find complete listings, locations and functions of all of the Russian infiltrators. It was all the evidence that they needed. Operation 'Clean Sweep' was quickly put into action and within hours nearly all those on the lists were in custody. The number of senior posts that were held by infiltrators was more than anyone had expected. After a massive enquiry and much vetting completed, Sir George sat in his office satisfied that everything in the corridors of power was now under control. A modicum of trust could return to the ministry but they must be alert to the possibility that a future attempt to replace the lost agents might occur.

After his short break from his office the Home Secretary announced that he was stepping down because of a medical condition. The Prime Minister accepted his resignation and the media had a field day on speculation about his replacement. Sometime later the Home Secretary disappeared and was believed to have been seen in the company of the K.G.B. many agents were exchanged at the bridge at Friedrich Strasse, Check Point Charlie, including the defection to the West of Werner Stiller. He had continued to help to identify others following the help given to find Bellinger. In Sir George's office he spoke to Freddy "Well done Freddy or should I now say Huntley. You opened Pandora's Box with your German antics and whoever would have thought that it would lead to what it did. There will be a 'Gong' in this coup for me in the near future and I am certain that you Huntley will be highly decorated for your outstanding contribution to national security. I would be very disappointed if you chose to leave us now. You have every right to if you choose but I do hope that you remain with us." "Thank you, sir, I can't see myself doing anything else now. I would be delighted to remain in the service." Freddy accepted. I am very pleased and I can now tell you that you are to be promoted to the rank of Commander and you will be sent for full training to fit you for your appointment. You will be away for some time but I look forward to your return." They shook hands in true respect and friendship. Freddy was soon sent to special traing and spent a lot of time in different countries familiarising himself with traditions and various activities associated with them. After many months of training, he returned to London to take up active service but first he was due a lot of leave and he decided to take a sabbatical in his home town. He felt that after he lost his identity, he needed to try to pick up the threads of his life again.

CHAPTER 7

Following the sixties spy scandal and the Cuba crisis, Huntley Haverstock returned to his former life as Freddy Goodchild. During his involvement in the 'D' notice affair with Cuba and the foreign spies, all records of Freddy's existence had been destroyed by the foreign agents. The British Secret Services had restored his records following extensive investigations. Freddy and his friend Master pilot Pinky James had given the secret services tremendous help in exposing infiltrators who had managed to establish themselves in many British Government departments. Only the government offices had any record of the help that they had given, it could never be in the public domain. Freddy did however hold an M.B.E. for outstanding courage and contribution to Her Majesties government. Many infiltrators in the Government services had been identified and arrested around the time of the Cuban crisis and many new security measures had been introduced. It was hoped that the new measures would prevent any such infiltration in the future.

Freddy's help at that time had been invaluable and was the main reason for his recognition. He had remained with the secret services for some time following that affair and had been trained and promoted in the service. He had been involved in a number of investigations but none as serious as his first. It seemed a long time after his joining the service and he was due leave. He was subject to recall as Huntley Haverstock when the service required him. It was a long time since he had seen his family who had believed him dead but unbeknown to Freddy his family had died in that time. The family were led to believe that Freddy had died because when they enquired about him, they were told that was no record of anyone of that name. He was now taking his leave and travelling home to Middlesbrough wondering what lay ahead on taking up his earlier life. As he left London on his way to Middlesbrough, he reflected that his circumstances were now totally different as he was now very wealthy and had the means to do what might have been unthinkable before. He travelled up the A1 in his Aston Martin DB4GT 'jet coupe' enjoying his 0-60miles per hour acceleration in 6.4 seconds. It was very gratifying to think that his wealth had mainly come from the people who had tried to kill him. He hadn't heard from family or friends but had had contact with his former R.A.F. associates. As he drove through the driving rain, he realised that he was quite nervous and apprehensive as he approached his home town.

Middlesbrough was an "Iron" town, built on the local requirements of the Dorman and Long steel works. Previous to the steel works the town was a half way stage between Whitby Abbey and Durham Cathedral. Monks would rest there on their journeys between the Priories and access the ferry across the Tees-river. "Would his house still be there or had it been sold off by the family?" "What would the family think when he walked in on them?" these were just a few of the things that haunted him as he pulled up outside of his house in Linthorpe. The rain had eased to a fine drizzle as he walked up the path and stopped outside of his front door. For the first time he had a look at the frontage, the windows were covered by metal sheets and the door was sealed up by boards screwed into the door frame. A sign read, 'DANGER DO NOT ENTER'. Freddy was not going to be told that he could not enter his own house, no matter who had put up the sign. Freddy was in shock as he slowly went back to his car to get a tyre lever and as he approached the front door he wondered if his keys would still fit or had the locks been changed as well.

He prized the board off across the lock and tried his key, it turned and he pushed the door open. The door resisted from lack of use but as it opened the smell from inside stung his nostrils and sent him reeling backwards. He covered his face with a handkerchief as he levered off the remaining boards from the door frame and he entered the house. Not one bit of furniture was left in the house, everything had been removed and the house was littered with smashed pots, flower jars, ornaments and paperwork. The house had been totally emptied of furniture and carpets. It looked as if looters had cleared the place of everything of use. What was that smell? The downstairs rooms had the appearance of desolation with dirt and mess spread all over the floors. What had happened here? After searching upstairs as well as down he eventually looked in the cupboard under the stairs and his gaze was met by a hollow-eyed corpse in an advanced state of decomposition. He was shocked but there seemed to be something familiar about it, the stained clothing indicated that whoever this was had been shot or stabbed in the stomach and left to die a slow death trapped under the stairs. Freddy checked the clothing for any identification but there was nothing. As he leaned across the corpse, he spotted a message written on the back of the door in blood: 'SECS has the answer'.

Freddy recalled that the only person who knew SECS, was his cousin John. This had to be poor John and the realisation made Freddy feel quite sick in his stomach. What was John doing here? John lived near Redcar and they hadn't seen each other since childhood. It did not make sense that John should meet his end in Freddy's house in Middlesbrough. The message referred to the answers being in the secret safe. When they were young boys, they had used the safe to keep their private things away from the girls and the adults that frequented the house. They kept their catapults and ammunition in there, their copies of 'naughty parchments' that parents must not see and their treasured copies of the Dandy and the Beano. Freddy went to the fireplace in the front room and with the help of the tyre lever he lifted the hearth stone, underneath was the steel safe unscratched. Freddy and John were the only people to know that the safe code was grandmother's birthday. Freddy opened the safe and inside there was just one item, a stringed bag. Opening the bag there was a letter stained with John's blood: 'As I write this, they are still in the house so I hope to get it in

SECS before they see me. They are looking for something but I don't know what. Your family thought that you were dead and they are now, you are alone. They beat me up but I told them nothing. Billy told me that you were still alive and I came to sort the family affairs and I knew that you would come for GG's box. Good Luck. John' Poor John thought Freddy and he remembered fondly the good times that they had together and the scrapes that they got into. He remembered with sad fondness. "So, who were these people and what are they after?" thought Freddy, "could they be to do with the Cuban affair? Are they a new security threat? I will check with Sir George. Freddy put the letter into his pocket and looked into the bag. There was a scarf wrapped around something quite solid but that was all there was. He unwrapped the scarf to find inside a small metal box. Freddy shook it and it contained something that rattled but there seemed to be no lid, no lock, no seams and so no way of getting into it. There was an inscription on the box that read: 'Albert Reuben 1865' . It meant nothing of significance to Freddy but he remembered that his great grandfather was called Albert Reuben but 1865? That must have been what John was referring to, GG's box. Freddy thought back to John's final warning, maybe the house was being watched and he may be being observed even now. He had better heed John's warning and get out quickly.

He left and headed for a safe house where he could contact Sir George. He made sure that he was not followed to the safe house and he arrived safely to find the house empty. Following a call to Sir George who was a departmental head of British Intelligence, Freddy was convinced that no security issues were involved. The only mystery was how to open the box to see what it contained and what was the significance of this strange box, after all it had cost his family and John their lives. He had to start by investigating 'Albert Reuben 1865'. 1865 must be important if it was Freddy's great grandfather then he had to find out about him. He left the safe house and headed for Stockton-on-Tees where his great Grandfather had lived before he moved to Park Lane in Middlesbrough. As he drove down the Stockton Road, he contemplated cutting open the hollow box but worried about the damage he may do to the contents. He was deep in thought when a black Mercedes drew alongside and as he glanced at it, he found himself looking down the barrel of a gun pointing right at him. The gunman was a front seat passenger who indicated that he wanted Freddy to pull over to the road side. In an instant his 'Jet Coupe' sprang into action, accelerating such that it left the Mercedes standing. Freddy tried to read the number plate in his rear-view mirror as he sped away but he only managed to get a part of it. He thought that it could be traced quite quickly as there were not too many cars of that sort in the north east of the country. The Mercedes faded into the distance and at the first opportunity, he left the road unseen around a bend. His training came to him automatically and he applied his knowledge to lose his followers.

Sure, that he was no longer being tracked he stopped and contacted Government security services on his car radio. They came back to him with three possible owners, one a doctor another a car dealer and the third an M.P. It was dark when he arrived in Stockton having taken a wide detour to lose his followers. He stopped outside of

Lol Davison's house. Lol and Freddy were childhood friends and Freddy hoped that, Lol still lived here and could put him up for the night. Lol opened the door and his mouth dropped open, "You are supposed to be dead. Great to see you, come in. What have you been up to? Where have you been all this time?" "I'll just park the car round the back, out of sight." Lol met Freddy as he parked the car and showed him in through the back door. "I know that it is a bit presumptuous, but could you put me up for the night?" "Of course," said Lol, "I have a spare room, come on I'll show you." They came back down to the lounge and Lol opened up a vintage bottle of wine. "You have arrived at a good time, I have just taken delivery of a few cases of Italian wines, you can help me test them out." Lol was full of questions because he had been told that Freddy had died while serving in the R.A.F. Freddy told him as much of events as he could but much of his story was still classified information. As the evening progressed, they relaxed and sampled the wines. They talked about the good old days when they were kids into the early hours of the morning. Lol was fascinated to find out what Freddy would do now and was very keen to help if he could. Freddy suggested that they sleep on it and take it up the next morning. They retired for the night. The following morning at breakfast, Freddy told Lol that he would take a room at the Swallow Hotel in Stockton. He thanked Lol for his help and assured him that he would keep him in touch and if he needed help, he would get back to him after he learned more about the box and why it was so important. The box, after all, had cost people their lives. He said that he would contact Lol as soon as he knew the room number at the Swallow and after he had booked in. With that Freddy left and headed for Stockton High Street.

Chapter 8

True to his word Freddy called Lol and told him his room number. Freddy did not fully unpack but he picked up the box to study it but could find no way of getting the thing open. There were no seams and no obvious construction signs but there was something inside which rattled when shaken. Freddy wrapped the box in a small face cloth and put it into his toiletry bag and took the bag to the front desk. He called for the Hotel manager and arranged for the bag to be placed inside the hotel safe with strict instructions that no other member of staff was to be informed of its existence and no one other than Freddy could collect it or be told about it being there. "What if you need it to be collected?" enquired the manager. "Unless I collect it in person, no one must know anything about it, is that clear. It is very important that you follow these instructions to the letter!" The manager assured Freddy that he would let no one other than himself open the safe and no one would be told that Freddy had deposited anything in the safe. Back in his room Freddy sat and thought about recent events and why people should be following him. It had to be the box that made him a target and that meant that the box had to have some great value. The people following would stop at nothing to get their hands on the box, that was clear but who were they? Freddy's thoughts were interrupted by the room telephone, it was Lol. "I am in a phone box just off the High Street and I need to see you urgently." Lol sounded very shaken, "What is the problem?" "My front door was smashed down and a gang burst into the house. I was out the back and escaped out of the garden door and climbed out over the garden fence. I can't go back they are still in there and from where I was, I could see that they were turning the house upside down. They were wrecking the place!" "Did they see you or know where you are?" asked Freddy. "No, I was out before they could possibly see me." "Which phone box are you in? Never mind, go round to the restaurant on Church Road and I will come and get you. Try and keep out of sight and watch for my car coming for you."

Freddy put the phone down and went to his car and headed for Church Road. He drove very slowly-along the road and he saw Lol run out of an alley way. Freddy opened the passenger down and without fully stopping he saw Lol jump in. They headed quite slowly without interfering with other road users and headed for the main road out of Stockton. After ten miles, it was clear that no pursuers had followed them. Slowly Freddy, drove back to the Swallow Hotel and they went to Freddy's room without being seen by anyone. "This is more-nasty than I ever could have imagined, what the hell is going on Freddy?" "I have very little idea at the moment but I think that it all has to do with the little box and whatever is inside of it." The phone rang and it was Sir George Curswell, the head of sercret services in London. Freddy answered and confirmed coded identities, "We have had some people making enquiries about Freddy Goodchild and we have been unable to establish who initiated the enquiries but they were made through a contracted enquiry agent who could not confirm who they were being paid by. We, of course denied any knowledge of a Freddy Goodchild and there was no reference to Huntley at all. We need to meet. I am in Leeds tomorrow can you be at the Leeds head-quarters about two in the afternoon?" "Of course, Sir George, I will be there." and as he replied the phone went dead. "Was that Sir George that did that or was the call intercepted?" thought Freddy.

He quickly packed his things and went to see the manager to let him know that he still required the room for an indefinite period but he would not be returning to occupy tonight. He picked up his bag and called for Lol and they set off for Leeds. Freddy was applying all his training to be sure of that they were not able to be followed. After much detouring and evasive manoeuvres, they arrived at the Wetherby Hotel and booked adjacent rooms. In the restaurant Freddy and Lol considered their situations, "I'm sorry to have involved you in this, whatever it is Lol." "From what I now know of the situation you could not have possibly foreseen such an aggressive and persistent group following you. The box doesn't look like any metal that I am aware of, it isn't gold, platinum or silver or even steel. I would never have thought that such a small metal box would be so valuable to someone that they would go to such desperate lengths." replied Lol. "Well, I have caused you to be temporarily homeless but I will be able after my meeting tomorrow to arrange a solution for you. In the meantime, let's try to have a pleasant evening while we have the chance. Do you still have contact with the crowd that we used to knock about with?" They talked well into the early hours about the old times and characters that they used to know. They enjoyed the hotel hospitality and the food and drink but eventually they retired for the night.

Freddy had an early start and left without waking Lol but he left a note to say the he would be back in the late afternoon. He headed for Leeds H.Q. as he had a lot of work to do before Sir George arrived. Records could provide some information that could throw some light on the metal box and it's origins and possibly the people who were trying to get their hands on it. In the records section he trawled through file after file with little success when Bert, one of the Leeds staff, came into the room with some information on metallurgical research which he thought might be of help. Freddy thanked Bert and opened the file to find the cover sheet describing the file content on metallurgy development programmes but the rest of the file was empty. All project information had been removed but there was a name at the top of the file cover, hardly distinguishable, which startled Freddy. The name was that of his great grandfather Albert Reuben Goodchild. He knew little of his family history but he knew the name well and that was all that he knew about his great grandfather. The rest of the file was blank apart from a few reference numbers that someone had attempted to obliterate. The file room door opened to reveal Sir George framed in the doorway, "There you are Huntley!" Sir George always used Freddy's code name. "What are you up to?" Freddy greeted him and suggested that they grab a coffee and find a private office. They settled down with their fresh coffees in a secured interview room with the door locked, "Have you found anything of significance Sir George?" "No but I think that you have a lot to tell me from your intensity, I had very little to go on." "Neither did I but Bert came up with this file, which you may find to be of interest." Freddy opened the file and passed it over to Sir George. He noticed the security level of the file and he was obviously astounded that a file of that level could have been compromised in such a way. "I will take this and make some enquiries. This is a very serious matter that must involve people with a high security clearance, tell me more about your story." Freddy spent a long time explaining all that had happened and how Lol had become involved. They talked for over an hour exploring all the possible scenarios or reasons for the past events but everything led back every time to the mysterious box. "I'll take the box to the boffins and see what they can make of it and come up with. As Lol appears to have been drawn into this, I will leave it up to you how much you involve him. In light of what has happened of late, you are now back on the pay role and you can allocate what is needed to accommodate Lol. This is now an official enquiry, Huntley Haverstock, so you are both bound to the regulations, so make Lol fully aware of all requirements." With that they set off to pick up Lol from the Wetherby Hotel and the box from the Swallow. On arrival at the Swallow Hotel the manager was in quite a state, Lol was trying to calm him down, I didn't tell them anything Mr. Goodchild but they wouldn't listen and they took your room key and tore the place apart, it is a total mess." "Did the safe contents come into the conversation?" "No, I said that you had kept yourself to yourself since you arrived and that I knew nothing about you. Who were they Mr. Goodchild? They were real nasty pieces of work." "I'm afraid that we do not know but we will make good any damages and I will take me package without delay and many thanks for your discretion, you did very well." Huntley settled the hotel bill and all three set off for London with the box safely in their possession. They left the cars at Leeds H.Q. and they were escorted in a security car to the Leeds rail station to complete their journey. They were met at Kings Cross station by a security team to ensure that no one knew of their arrival or journey through London. It was a pleasant day as they travelled and they were sufficiently relaxed after their rail journey to take in the views as they headed for Sir George's office. On arrival Sir George offered them the office suite accommodation which they both gracefully accepted. Freddy had stayed there before when he and Pinky James had helped security previously. Freddy explained to Lol that the suites were five-star accommodation and fully stocked with refreshments. Lol was very pleased with his room, he had never seen such luxury. Sir George left them and set off with the box to the scientific development department. After Sir George left Freddy and Lol discussed the immediate future. "Look I didn't expect to involve you in this mess, Lol but now that you are we need to decide if you want to get out now or become even more involved." "It is a no brainer I'm not letting these thugs get away with trashing my home and causing so much distress. It is now that mates need to stand up and be counted and I am standing up. What do you want me to do?" "I don't know yet but it is great to have you on board. I will get Sir George to make you legit with salary and a place you can call for now. You can if you want to stay in one of the billets in London if you prefer. The billets are very good, I have one near here on the Embankment, I can get you in there if you would like that." Lol nodded. "Okay that's settled we'll take a stroll round there now. I will let security know what we are doing so Sir George can get in touch." They walked along Whitehall and called in to pick up a car from the security garages. They continued by car to the Embankment billets. When they arrived, Freddy got the keys from the attendant and showed Lol his new quarters. Lol was very impressed and after a full tour of the place they set off by car to Bond Street to do some serious shopping. It was a new experience for Lol to charge everything to an account that someone else would settle for him so he bought one or two things for the sheer hell of it. London was new to Lol so Freddy gave him an extensive tour of the city 'up west' and points of interest. They enjoyed a coffee in the '2 i's' coffee bar in Soho where Freddy introduced him to the resident singers Vince Eager, Wee Willy Harris and Ricky Towns. They walked through Piccadilly to

Leicester Square, on to St. James Park and back to Whitehall. They enjoyed the walk as the sun was warm for an autumn day and there was no wind. When they got back, they had to cool down for a while before going to Sir George's office. As they entered, they were greeted by Sir George, "Well! What do those boffins get paid for? I've no idea, not one of them could get anywhere with that confounded box of yours. They tried to cut it, burn it, hammered it and even tried to open it with acids. Not even a scratch on it and it just rattled at them. None of them has any idea about its' contents. What have you two been up to?" "I have booked Lol into an Embankment billet near mine, done some shopping and taken in some of the local points of interest. I take it that the box provided no answers?" "Nothing," was the reply, "So Lol has decided to see this through for the time being so we will have to put him on the team, if that is okay with you." "They were also my thoughts," said Freddy, "he will be working with me so I will arrange all necessary training and instruction, is that okay with you Sir?" "Yes, that's fine but I can't help you in where to start. These people have left us without any clues as any leads have been a dead end at contractors who haven't a clue. It is up to you to get going. I will allocate a team for you to use as back-up or researchers. We have ensured that your John has a decent burial. My office and resources are ready to support you when needed as this smacks of our enquiries on one of joint previous cases. National security might be again at risk. Go to it lads and keep me informed." "Thank you, Sir we will keep in full communication." With that they left and walked back to the Embankment but the weather had changed for the worse and they were relieved to sit down to a terrific Italian meal at the restaurant adjacent to their billets overlooking Westminster bridge.

CHAPTER 9

It was nice for Freddy to meet the restaurant staff again and renew old friendships. As they ate Freddy mulled over the possible starting points of enquiry and decided that he should start with finding all he could about Albert Reuben Goodchild. They finished their meal and at the records office Freddy trawled through the files and found that Albert had worked in the Dorman and Long research and development department at the Lackenby Steel works in Middlesbrough. He had specialised in Bessimer Steel sampling but that is where all traces stopped. No references, no further information and missing files content. The last entry referred to 1897. Someone had been through this information and for some reason taken all further relevant documentation. In another section Freddy found that in the same year as the last entry Albert has disappeared. There were no reports of accidents, deaths or travel details. It was as if he had left the planet Earth never to be seen again. No wonder the family history was so sparse and full of supposition and myth. So it all led to the Middlesbrough Steel works and that was where they had to start.

The very next day they visited Jackie Beal who worked in the I.C.I. metallurgy department. He told them of an old co-operation that had been established years ago on a project that had been abandoned. He told them that the only place that might have some information would be at Lackenby works. Now they had a starting point but hey had to be prepared for anything in the future so they went to a local weapons section and collected a full weapons pack, just in case. They had travelled by train to Leeds and had collected Freddy's car to drive on to Middlesbrough and there they had booked into the Highfield Hotel. It was late as they drove back through lashing rain to the hotel and the north east wind forced them to have the car heating on full blast.

Freddy commented that the north was always a few degrees colder than London and the south but even he was shocked at the change in conditions. They certainly would not like to walk anywhere in this sort of weather. After a good night's sleep and a hearty breakfast, they set off on the dull Sunday morning to visit Don Fielding, a friend of Lol, who also worked at one time at I.C.I. along with Jackie. He lived on the Beechwood Estate. Freddy was alert to anyone who may be following them but he was sure that they were alone. The estate was very quiet, as always on a Sunday morning. Freddy parked the car on a field behind Don's house and they walked through the cut into the housing. Lol knocked at the door but it was some time before there was any answer. Lol thought that Don might not be at home but after a few more knocks the door opened to reveal someone who had had a very good night out and was showing the after effects. "Good grief! I thought it was ghosts, I haven;t seen you two for years, what's up? Come in and find a place to sit, if you can. They both knew their way around the house and they went into the lounge. A body came to life on the settee, rubbed it's eyes and staggered out of the front door. "Who was that?" asked Lol. "No idea!" said Don who was busy in the kitchen trying to find everything needed to make a cup of tea. The place was a mess. "Good party?" "I think so," said Don, "I will let you know later when I wake up a bit." Don came into the lounge. He had managed to make the tea and even found some biscuits. "Help yourselves, I couldn't be responsible for pouring tea this morning." As he spoke Don threw some debris on the floor to make room for a sit down and he flopped into an arm chair. The teas were poured and Freddy made some small talk before asking Don about metallurgy and in particular the qualities that applied to research in the nineteenth century at I.C.I. "Funny you should ask about that. Is it important?" "It has cost people their lives and may be of national security." "When I was working in the R & D section at I.C.I. Wilton, I came across an old enquiry from a team at Dorman and Long. I took particular notice because I saw the name Goodchild on the file cover. A relation of yours?" Freddy nodded. "It appears that Dorman and Long labs were asking I.C.I. to confirm some incomplete steel particulars. The file reply was strange in that they said no tests were conclusive but then they refused them any further help. That is just not like any I.C.I. response to possible development material. They would be falling all over themselves to develop and pinch it if it showed promise but just to dismiss and enquiry of that nature was not an I.C.I. option that I would think of. I looked into it but couldn't find anything in our archives about it. All things like that were recorded and kept but there was nothing. Wait, Old Stan Barker would have worked there about that time and his grandson has just retired from the same department as him. Now he lives on Sutton Estate just over the field there. I have his address somewhere." "that's great Don, we need to speak to him as soon as possible." Don left the room and soon returned with an address. They thanked him and apologised for disturbing his Sunday morning snooze time and they left. They assured Don that they would be in touch again and let him know what had happened. Don was quite excited as they left to see Stan's grandson, his recovery was remarkable.

As they approached the address they had been given, the door opened and Alan Barker was about to leave. He came to a halt as he turned and saw the two boys approaching. Alan was not in a co-operative mood but Freddy explained why they were calling on him and Freddy was not going to be put off by the frosty welcome. He took out his official security card and displayed it for Alan to see. The change was dramatic from being aggressive and uncooperative to a fearful character who had something to hide. He re-entered the house, followed by Freddy and Lol. No words were spoken but it wasn't necessary as Alan's nerve snapped and he started to bluster and deny everything and anything. Freddy stared at him and eventually Alan went on to admit that he had passed on some industrial information but under great pressure. "Stop there!" said Freddy, "what information and to who?" "It was only that one time, three guys demanded that I pass them a Dorman and Long enquiry sheet that was in a file that I was working on. They said that something really nasty would happen to me if I did not do as they said. They were big lads all of them so I didn't argue. That's all!" "Who were these guys?" "Some contractor who I had seen on site who worked from his shed in Grangetown. He is called Gordon Trattles. I had no choice. What else could I do? It wasn't important stuff, anyway, it was only a Dorman and Long steel enquiry." "Just important enough to get people killed. Where's your phone? Alan pointed to the hall. Freddy called the local police identifying himself with the operation code and had Alan taken away for further interrogation. Lol had done some building work with Trattles and was fully aware that he had dealings with the criminal fraternity. "We may need back up at this point Lol so we may have to delay going after this guy until it arrives.

 They made their way back to the Highfield Hotel and had some lunch. The sun shone on the hotel gardens as Freddy considered how long it would take for Sir George to get back to him. He had left a message for him but he thought that the office weekend programme would mean that he would not hear from him until after lunch on Monday. Meetings with the ministers on Monday morning always took priority and always lasted until they took lunch, no matter how trivial the subject matter was. As

Freddy and Lol were leaving the next morning a member of the hotel staff gave Freddy a message from the local police. It read, 'the contractor had been collecting the information on behalf of a professor Pescolari who is based in Geneva at the Fontain & Brach laboratories. "A lead at last and it takes us to Geneva. We have no further need to bother the local contractor. I'll let H.Q. know and we can take a little weekend relaxation. How about going to Redcar and striking up old acquaintances at some of the old haunts?" Lol agreed and they set off for the coast. Redcar had not changed much since Freddy had last spent some time there. Everything was in full swing on the Sunday morning. The ghost train and other amusements were doing great business. Screams emanated from the interior of the ghost train and not all were children's screams. As they queued up to get an ice cream, Lol spotted a familiar face in the crowd, "Don't look now but outside of the rock shop is one of the men who trashed my house!" "We'll get our ice creams and walk up the sea front to the street near the R.N.L.I. life boat station. We can hide in the cut through to the high street and see if he follows us. Having got their ice creams, they casually strolled up the sea front and turned into the alleyway leading to the high street. As soon as they turned the corner, they ran twenty or so yards to a alleyway junction. Freddy went left and Lol right. Seconds passed before they heard the approaching sound of hurried steps. As he follower got level with the junction Lol shouted and the man turned to face him. Freddy tackled him from behind and took the man to the floor with a resounding crash. For the first time ever, Freddy used his hand cuffs to restrain someone. He had bound the man with hands behind his back. "I'll hold him until you get back Lol, dial 999 and get the police here as quick as you can. Tell them it is a code MS." Lol ran to the high street but found that the call box was damaged so he went to the Red Lion hotel where the manager was very helpful and before Lol could get back to Freddy, he could already hear the approaching police sirens showing that their response to his call had been extremely rapid. The man was taken into custody and the Chief Constable was informed that the secret services would be in touch to take the prisoner as soon as possible. Another message went to Sir George informing him of the situation. The Chief Constable was not too happy but after his questions were answered he complied without any further objections. The prisoner carried no identification and refused to make any comment or answer any questions. Freddy insisted that the man was to be charged with aggravated burglary and that he should be held until he was taken by security. Freddy addressed the Chief Constable, "Thank you for your co-operation and I am sure that he is safe in your custody. We haven't time to waste on his sort and he will be taken where he will answer the charges." They left Redcar headed back to the Highfield Hotel where they checked out and headed back to London. They were sure that they weren't followed but just to be certain they detoured and took standard evasive procedures.

CHAPTER 10

Back at the Embankment they were just in time to join Mario in a great meal in the cafe before retiring for the night after a very busy day. Freddy left information for Sir George before falling into a welcome, deep but disturbed sleep. The next morning, they were taking breakfast in Antonio's cafe when they were approached by a messenger from Sir George with news of the prisoner left in custody with the Redcar police, he was dead! He had been found dead that very morning hanging in his cell. No further information had been given. The messenger left them both shocked and confused as they considered how a prisoner could be allowed to have the means to kill himself whilst in custody, that is assuming it was suicide. "Who and what are we dealing with for a man to take his life over such a menial charge. It doesn't make sense when any lawyer, worth the title, would have had him out of jail in minutes and probably with only a caution. There has to be something about this that we haven't discovered, so important for such drastic behaviour. It can only mean that there is a lot of money at stake somehow. Sir George told me that the boffins could not make any impression on the box, not even a scratch. That leads me to think that the contents are not as important as the box itself. The properties and composition of the box must be the target of this group following us about. Our professor Pescolari must have some ideas about it. I'll go to H.Q. but if you want to stay and have a wander…." Lol cut him off in mid-sentence, "No! I'm with you, I need to know what this is about as much as you do." "Okay, let's go to the records department and see if they can come up with something on this Pescolari chap." When they arrived at records Henry already had made some important findings on the professor. It was confirmed that Pescolari was a leading metallurgical chemist working for the F.A.K. Foundation based in Geneva. "So, it looks as if we are on the right track at last. We need to go over to Geneva and meet this guy face to face and see what he knows about the box. We will go to the office and update Sir George." Lol nodded in agreement. Sir George could not allocate any agents from his post in the U.K. but he agreed to alert any agents in the area of Geneva to the investigation and ask for any relevant knowledge to be relayed back to the U.K. They had no way of setting a plan but they knew that backup was available if required. They both agreed that the best approach would be to meet the professor at his home for the best results but everything depended on his response. They were packed very quickly and on the way to the airport for the flight to Geneva, a driver had been sent to pick them up. Pescolari worked in Geneva and after they arrived in the afternoon, they picked up their hire car and headed for the Quai Gustave Ador where the professor worked. They had some photographs of him but they were quite old copies and they hoped that he could still be recognised from them. They passed the Quai Gustave and headed for the house in Avenue De L'Aurore. Freddy drove passed the house to see if there were any signs of life but all was quiet so he parked a little way away in the Avenue Du Printemps. They parked and waited for the professor to arrive home. Freddy hoped that the information on the professor was correct and that his English was good as Freddy could speak some French but it was far from fluent. After, waiting for a while Freddy felt that things were being left to chance by just waiting. They had to have the element of surprise and that could not be achieved from the car. "Come on, we are going in. We will leave the car here and walk to his house before he gets home. That gives him less chance of spotting us and doing a runner." Lol nodded and they headed for the house. It was a three-story building with metal fences and a large metal gate which opened smoothly. They checked for people watching as they entered the gates but it was a very quiet area and there was no one in sight. The front day was locked so they walked slowly around the house until they spotted a window which was slightly open. It was a small window but large enough when opened for Lol to lean inside and open the large window beside it. Once inside they closed the window and started to look around the house. The main bedrooms were downstairs along with a bathroom and toilet. Upstairs was a large sitting room with excellent views of the front of the building. No one could approach the house without being seen from the sitting room. It overlooked the large gate and it gave a panoramic view of the road outside. They settled down to wait but they did not need to wait long before a car stopped and parked outside of the gate. The driver got out and came through the big gate and approached the door. From the photographs they recognised that the driver was indeed professor Pescotari. They heard the key in the front door lock and the door opening and closing, then footsteps on the stairs. Freddy stood behind the sitting room door and Lol stood flat against the wall on the other side. The professor opened the door and walking over to the side table. He heard the door close behind him and turned to find himself facing two strangers. "Please do not be alarmed professor we do not mean you any harm or discomfort, we just need to talk to you." The professor sank slowly onto the settee, clearly in shock. "We are sorry to startle you in this way but we are only here to ask you about the men that you hired in the U.K. We are investigating certain matters on behalf of Her Majesties Services and we need your help." It took some time for the professor to recover his composure and comprehend the situation.

Freddy and Lol seated themselves opposite the professor and waited for a response. "How did you get into my house?" he asked.

"You left a window open. I must explain, as I said previously, that we are acting on behalf of the U.K. Government in respect to murder and serious assault associated with another very serious matter." "I have nothing to do with such things. The people I hired said that they were private investigators. I needed someone in the U.K. to be able to access information on a company called I.C.I. I made it clear that they should respect the Laws of the U.K. but if they could find me any information on a rumour that a metal had been discovered that could be changed or altered without the use of heat or chemicals then they would be well rewarded. The notion of such a metal is ludicrous but I had to follow up on it as the financial and commercial benefits would be outstanding. They assured me that they knew of this and could find proof of such a metal, so I paid them a handsome sum of money to pay any expenses. My employer was only to pleased, to back me with the necessary finances. You mentioned murder, surely these people were not involved?" Freddy thought for a while, going back over the conversation with Alan and the pressure that he had been under at the time. Freddy concluded that there was no evidence of any wrong doing.

The Redcar suicide man had no apparent connection to them. The professor interrupted his thoughts, "I will take you to talk to my employer, Monsieur Le Blanc if you wish and he will confirm all that I have told you. After a short pause Freddy said "I do not think that it will be necessary to do that, we are sorry to have met you in such a manner but before we leave you, we will need the paper that they sent to you." The professor immediately got up and opened his brief case, taking a paper from it he handed it to Freddy. The professor said, "We found nothing of value in the report to support or explain the attributes so you are very welcome to take it but it did give some validation to the claim that such a metal does exist." "Thank you, professor we will leave you in peace and hope that we did not cause you too much distress." The professor assured them that he understood as he accompanied them to their car. They parted in congenial terms. When they reached the airport Freddy contacted Sir George to keep him up to date with their progress.

They caught the evening flight to London. Lol was surprised that Freddy had taken Pescotti at his word but Freddy explained that the information on the I.C.I. report was as much as they now needed and though there might be some doubt about Pescotti, it could wait. When they arrived at Sir Georges' office, he was busy reading the I.C.I. report and Freddy joined him. The name at the top was Albert but there was also a reference number which was hand written. Most of the report was typed. No information was helpful as to the nature of the metallurgical enquiry and there were no details of any formula. In faint pencil at the bottom, barely legible, was "ref to me". "I wonder what that is" pondered sir George. "Who is me, I wonder." said Freddy. "I will get records on to that straight away". Sir George picked up the phone and gave instructions there and then. "We will wait for a response." "Tea, coffee?" They sat drinking their coffee and related past events expressing possibilities but it was becoming very clear that there were two factions involved, one, obviously more desperate and violent than the other. They had no clues as to who the second group were. It wasn't long before the phone rang and Sir George answered. "It appears M.C. is the project manager in charge at that time". He died some years ago but his grandson was working at I.C.I. quite recently. He is called Jason Condor after his grandfather Martin Jason Condor. It looks as if we have a possible line of enquiry." The report from records showed that there was lots of information relating to Jason Condor. He had been named as a member of a number of suspect groups which had led to a number of criminal convictions. The latest five showed two convictions for fraud, one for serious theft and two involving grievous bodily harm. He was not known for operating alone, he was constantly involved in some sort of gang activity. There was no record of a fixed address and he had not been known to be active for some time in fact there was no record of him being in the United Kingdom at this time. Strangely, there was no record of him having left the country. He had become a ghost figure. "It looks as if we've hit the jackpot Huntley." said Sir George. "It is a definite lead, Lol and I will start a trace on him. Can you find if there are any recent cases in England that fit his Modus Operandus? We'll go to last place he was sighted and take it from there."

Back in records Freddy found that the last address for Condor was Park Road South in Middlesbrough. Freddy and Lol made their way back to the Tees Valley and started making enquiries door to door and came across someone who had known him well. "Yes, I know Jason, we were good mates and regulars vat the Park Hotel." "What is your name?" "Sorry, I'm Bill Noakes." "We are trying to find out what happened to Jason and where he is now. Do you know where we can find him?" "I'm glad that someone is taking this seriously. I reported Jason missing ages ago. You said that you are from security services?" Freddy nodded. "Jason was really excited. He told me that he had hit the jackpot and would soon have more money than we had all ever seen. The last time that I saw him he was on his way to South Bank to meet some 'High Rollers' as he called them. We never saw or heard from him again." "Have you any idea who he was meeting?" "All that he said was that they were foreign guys and they were all millionaires and he had something that they would pay a lot of money for."

"Any idea what?" enquired Lol. "Something that he had found out about at work. He was a Lab assistant at I.C.I. I can't tell you any more about it because he kept close to his chest. He was always after the big breaks and he wasn't particular how he got it. One thing that might help and I've always kept it, it was the last thing connecting me with Jason, is the book of matches with the meeting time on it. Here you can have it if it helps you find him." "Thank you for your help. We will let you know if we find him." Freddy and Lol left Bill after he gave them the book of matches. The logo on the matches was Wilton social club, so that was where they headed.

Many years ago, Freddy had been a guest at the club, he had been invited to play golf and squash by a former member. He had been impressed by the many facilities that the club provided for it's members but on the social side, there had been indications of rifts between members and talk of underhand and devious dealings. Freddy had not changed his opinion since those times and he always regarded the place with deep suspicion. The membership had been very closed to outsiders and visitors had been treated with resentment and a dismissive attitude, distinctly unfriendly. Their investigations were not going to be easy or straight forward, they would need help from a present-day member. Lol was a great help in this matter as he was still in contact with his tradesmen friends who had contacts with the I.C.I. club, one who actually lived in Redcar.

Chapter 11

Redcar is a sea side resort on the north east coast. The arcades and pleasure rides were plentiful when Freddy and Lol were children. They remembered the Rock shop that made and sold Redcar Rock and the icecream parlours where the luxurious "Knickerboca Glories" could be savoured and enjoyed. With these memories in mind, they headed for the Red Lion Hotel to book a couple of rooms for the night. It had been many years since they both went riding at the Lobster horse riding stables, so after they got their room keys, they headed for the Lobster Inn.

It was a public house that had regular local support but was popular for visiting clients. At the rear of the pub there were extensive stables and horses owned by the Lobster but many kept their horses stabled there. It was early evening but they hadn't eaten all day so on arrival they ordered the Lobster Inn special, fish and chips. The fish was caught fresh every day and bought from the fishing Cobles on the Redcar beach. They were delicious and not one word was spoken until they had both cleared their plates. They washed the meal down with a pint of bitter and spent a pleasant evening remembering the good times they had and sadly commented on the fact that the stables had been gone such a long time. They would not be galloping down the beach again on Lobster horses. As they soaked up the atmosphere Lol attracted Freddy's attention to someone entering the bar. It was Don Fisher, the one that they had come to try and find. "That's a stroke of luck, Freddy, Don has found us and nothing could be more natural on our meeting him." Lol got up and approached the bar at the same time as Don. "It's Don, isn't it? Fancy meeting you after all this time. I'm here with my friend Freddy over at the table there." Lol pointed towards Freddy. "I don't know if you two have met before but let's get our drinks and join him at the table. Don approached the table, "Pleased to meet you Freddy" shaking Freddy's hand, "I never expected to see Lol here tonight, what a chance, eh? I don't think I have seen Lol since we converted the Alexander Hotel into flats." "Yes" said Lol "Freddy helped me out on that job with the electric wiring." "Great, so you are in the trade as well Freddy?" "No, just a 'go-for' for Lol." "What are you two doing in Redcar then?" "We were just slumming and reminiscing about the old riding school so we thought that we would come and see what it is like now." said Lol. "Sorry to say that the stables were demolished years ago." said Don, "It just wasn't paying its' way anymore and the boss here had no choice but to close it and extend the bar space." They continued chatting about the jobs that they had done together for some time. Lol steered the conversation, eventually, to the I.C.I. Social club. "Last time I was there I partnered Jason Condor in a golf four, do you ever get there now Don?" "I will be there tomorrow in a squash match. Do you want to come and give me some support?" "That would be fun, are we both invited?" "Of course, shall we say six-o-clock tomorrow evening? Look it's been great seeing you again and chatting about old times but that's my date that has just come in so I will see you both tomorrow, cheers lads."

Freddy looked at Lol and said, "How well do you know Fisher?" "Oh, he is okay. We have done lots of work together and he has always been reliable, why do you ask?" "I'm not sure, there was just something that wasn't right about that guy and the way he greeted us. You are probably right, maybe I am just being over sensitive. We are dealing with some very dangerous people and you never know how far their influence can reach." They finished their drinks and set off to walk back to the Red Lion Hotel. As they approached the front entrance there was a sudden movement in the shadows of the alleyway. Freddy reacted quickly and ran into the shadows where he had seen the movement but there was no one to be seen and no signs of anything out of place. Lol ran after him, "What was it?" "I don't know there is nothing to see now but I'm sure that someone was there watching us arrive." "You are just spooked, I didn't see anything." "Yes you are probably right, let's get inside away from this cold sea breeze which doesn't help."

The following day was spent sight-seeing and losing money in the 'one armed bandits' in the arcades. After a tea of the local fish and chips they set off for the I.C.I. Club to meet Don and he was waiting for them as they drove up to the club car park. "I'm glad that you are early there's just enough time to have a snifter in the members' bar." Don led the way into a very comfortable bar area and went round behind the bar and poured three drinks. After sitting down with their whiskies Don went on about his forthcoming match as the boys drank their drinks.

CHAPTER 12

Freddy woke up to find himself laid on a very lumpy and uncomfortable camp bed. He had no idea where he was or how he had got there. He looked around to see Lol laid on a table. He could hear voices and realised that people were in another adjoining room. He looked around for a door and there was just the one in the room that the boys had been put. Freddy heard someone say "They should be out for the count for another good half hour with the dose that Don gave them." Other voices were quite muffled and muted. Freddy got to Lol and shook him. It took a few minutes for him to come round. They discussed their situation and Freddy informed Lol about the comment from the next room. They were in a sports store room and there were no windows. The only light was from a dirty sky light in the ceiling. They knew that they had to get out and get away as fast as they could and they could distinguish about five different voices in the other room which made it unlikely that they could overpowering that number of captors. They seemed to waited an age before they heard a voice say, "That sounds like the boss has arrived. You two wait here while Jed and I go to meet him." "Is that wise, there's two of them in there and only two of us here?" "They will still be dead to the world for some time yet." A door slammed shut and they heard someone say "Grindley will be pleased with us when he sees that we have those two in there." "Quick Lol, get on your table and moan as if you are not much longer for this world." Lol got on the table and started moaning like a cow in agonising labour, Freddy was even concerned that Lol was actually in pain.

There was a cupboard behind the door which would give height advantage. Grabbing a hockey stick he climbed up behind the door. "Louder." said Freddy. There was a commotion aand some argument next door but Freddy heard the lock turn in the door and it opened to reveal two men. Lols' moaning and thrashing commanded both of their attention. As they moved towards Lol Freddy timed his attack to perfection. His feet landed on the back of the first one sending him smashing into the squash racket shelves while catching the other one with a mighty blow on the back of his neck. He went down and stayed down. Freddy quickly recovered his balance and quickly got to the other man but he was also unconscious. "Come on Lol, let's get out of here." They locked the stock room door behind them, leaving the two sleeping men inside and went out through the opposite door in the outer room. They found themselves in the squash court corridor and the emergency exit was straight ahead of them. Once outside they made their way around to the rear of the social centre and then onto the car park. A group of men were near Freddy's car, it had to be the gang and the tall man giving instructions had to be Gimly or Grindley, the boss. They heard the boss say, "Take me to them, there will be no distractions this time and we will have that box. You two get the car keys and hide their car, we don't want any nosy parkers asking silly questions." The group headed for the social club entrance and the boys watched as they disappeared through the club door. The boys came up behind the two men left in the car park and they took them completely by surprise. The men were left stunned and shocked as they grabbed the car keys and dashed to the car which started immediately and they headed off as fast as they could. "That was a lucky escape, Freddy, you certainly sorted those two out in the stock room it could have been very bad for us if we hadn't escaped when we did." "I couldn't afford to mess it up, we need to get to a safe house straight away.

I will get someone to pick up our gear from the Red Lion and I need to inform Sir George of the situation. We now have a definite lead there was something very familiar about that Grimly or Grindly guy." As they headed for the safe house, Lol went very quiet and Freddy realised that shock had set in with Lol. After all he was not trained or even used to such happenings. Freddy was conscious that Lol had fully realised how serious this was and it was certainly no game. These guys play for keeps. Freddy pulled into a farm entrance just outside of Ilkley and drove straight into a barn. He got out and closed the barn doors so that no prying eyes could see the car. They went into the farm house. The far was deserted and looked very run down from the outside but inside it had every facility one could think of. Freddy located the service radio set and opened the emergency channel, which sprang into life immediately. After a short delay Freddy heard Sir George respond and quickly confirmed identification. Freddy gave a full report of recent events including his suspicions about the boss called Grimly or whatever his name was. Sir George told Freddy to stay at the farm and he would send help as soon as he could. Freddy signed off and as he did, he remembered the vehicle parked in the middle of the car park at the social club. He couldn't be absolutely certain but he would wait for Sir George before he took any further action. They concentrated on settling down for the time being and set about making themselves comfortable.

Freddy asked Lol if he was going to stay with him on this mission, knowing that Lol had been badly shaken by events. "I think that things are getting a bit too intense for me and I haven't seen my uncle Joe in France for a long time." "I fully understand Lol and I think that it is a wise move to get out of the country for a while. You have been a great help to me and I appreciate all that you have done but enough is enough. When this is all over, we will meet up again and have a great vacation on the company funds. I will arrange all the necessary travel for your visit to France, you won't need to worry about anything. The company owes you. It would be wise not to go back to Stockton and your place until we find and deal with these people and bring them to justice. Best to stay here until arrangements are complete and then you can set off without being concerned that anyone has spotted you." "How soon can you arrange it, Freddy?" "Give me an hour."

Freddy went to the radio and contacted H.Q. And came back within half an hour to find Lol fast asleep. Best thing for him thought Freddy. He left him to sleep to get over some of the shock. Freddy left the paperwork and full itinerary for Lols' forthcoming journey to France. It was arranged that he would leave this evening and be in France tonight with a secure escort. The escort arrived within the hour and Lol was taken to Leeds Bradford airport in secret to board without delay on a charter flight to France. Lol found that a complete set of luggage had been provided. Freddy waved a fond farewell to Lol as the aircraft took to the skies and then he headed back to the farm. As he approached, he could see lights at the farm house. Freddy got close enough to see people searching from room to room. Freddy circled the building and saw two vehicles parked out of sight a short distance from the farm, obviously they did not want to be seen from the road as anyone approached the safe house. It had to be Grimlys' men or whatever his name was. The farm was surely not safe anymore. What to do? Challenge them? Not a good idea! Sneak up and try to identify some of them? How did they know where he was? Freddy sat in his car with his brain churning away at all the possibilities when he saw seven or eight men leaving the farmhouse and making their way back to their waiting vehicles. It was already quite dark and Freddy decided to turn the tables on them and follow to see where they were based or to whom they were reporting.

He reversed his car into a farm track entrance and waited. Soon he saw the headlights getting closer and he hoped that he had hidden he car sufficiently to go unnoticed. The cars passed and he could see as they did that no one even glanced his way. He followed them without turning on his car lights so as not to be seen following. They were not too far ahead and their lights on full beam lit the road very well for Freddy not to need his lights. They eventually left the minor roads and headed onto the M1. Dropping back a little before he got to the M1, Freddy turned on his own lights. Much to his surprise the group headed south and did not vary from that heading at all. As time progressed it became clear that they were heading for London. Freddy's mind buzzed with questions and possibilities as to who these people were and where they were heading. He followed them through London and he was shocked to say the least when he realised that they were directly headed for the Government buildings. As they entered White Hall Freddy passed the entrance and stopped a short distance away. He noticed that they group was not even challenged as they went through the check in gate.

Freddy headed for Sir George at his office. Sir George was not there so Freddy occupied one of the suites at the office and spent the night there. He did not sleep much as the gravity of this development left him wondering if his previous experiences of infiltrators were to be repeated. It was now very obvious that the leaks were within the organisation and that is how they knew where he was at all times after past reports to H.Q. He had a fitful night and hardly slept but he washed and shaved before sir George arrived shortly before eight-o-clock. It was Sir George's turn to be shocked to see Freddy sat in his desk chair as he entered. "Before you say anything, Sir George, I want to know how the so-called gang knew that I was at the safe house?" "What? Where's Lol?" "I sent him away yesterday." "What do you mean, they knew where you were? Did you get followed?" "No one followed me, they were given the information from H.Q. And they arrived in force. How else could they have known and so quickly.?" "You are not suggesting that I gave them the information? Freddy did not answer. "I certainly did not pass any information to any third party." "We have been in this situation before, Sir George, only you and I knew where we were, not just you, I contacted H.Q. to make arrangements for Lol to travel. We have a 'mole' in the department." "After our last purge I know that we have no one here who would leek information outside of the service." "Exactly!" Freddy went on to tell him why he was back in London and that the assailants were here in central London. Sir George sat down with a thump. "Are you telling me...." "Yes, I am. We have a very violent and determined organisation within this building trying to get their hands on that box, which I want back in my hands without delay." "I have it safe here." said Sir George. "Nothing is safe here. I want it back now." Sir George did not argue, he went straight to his personal safe and handed the box to Freddy. "I have a lot of checking to do, Sir George, if you want to come for an Italian meal about seven this evening at my embankment house, I will be able to tell you more." With that, Freddy left the office to make his enquiries.

At seven-o-clock precisely Sir George knocked on the door, "Come in Sir, Italian food as promised from downstairs, enjoy." A few pleasantries were exchanged during the meal but not a lot was said. As they finished their meal and washed it down with some Montipulciano Da Bruzzo Freddy started to tell of his findings. "I managed to identify those men who followed me and who I followed back here, they are all genuine Service men who were following orders from a Captain Simmerby, I misheard when I thought it was Grimley. He is part of the research department team and is head of research into metals. It all starts to make some sort of sense until one considers that they are willing to kill to get their hands on the box, including service personnel. They knew full well that I was a member of you team but I was a target." "Well, I have some news for you. After you left my office this morning my personal safe was broken into while I was out. You were right when you said that nothing was safe here. Who dares to give orders to break into my office and breach security protocol. If it is this Simmerby chap, I'll have his guts for garters." Sir George picked up the phone in Freddy's room and demanded to see Simmerby. Simmerby was his junior service member by a number of grades and Sir George was in the mood to tear Simmerby to pieces, probably to end his career in the service. Back at the office Simmerby was waiting for Sir George who gathered himself before inviting him in. "Sit down Simmerby I have a few questions for you." "Of course, sir, how can I help you? It is great to meet you at last" Freddy mused that it could be his last. Sir George continued, "you have been up north recently, might I ask what you were doing there?" "I was following your instructions Sir." "What instructions?" "Is it wise to discuss it here Sir?" He glanced at Freddy. "I asked you what instructions Simmerby and when I ask a question I want a reply." He was visibly having trouble keeping his temper with this man. Simmerby sensed the danger, "You ordered my team and I to obtain some box by any means required. You said it was of national security and that anyone who obstructed was to be eliminated." "Did you kill Freddy's cousin John?" "We had to deal harshly with him as he would not co-operate." "And the house in Stockton?" "We thought that it might be hidden there, Sir." "Did you also pursue Huntley Haverstock here and threaten his life?" "Those were your orders Sir." I gave you no such instructions Simmerby and you had better start telling me hwo you dare to act in such a way." "But sir, I have your written orders including breaking into your safe to get the box." Sir George was silent but obviously struggling with his anger and frustration. "You say that you have written instructions and orders from Sir George, can you confirm this?" asked Freddy. Simmerby showed his resentment at being questioned by Freddy but he sulkily nodded. Sir George called for the security, waiting outside of his office door, "You will escort Simmerby to his office and return with him here as soon as you can. Do not let him out of your sight. Simmerby, you need to produce your evidence. You will go with security and return here with your written orders, now!"

Security marched Simmerby out of the office and they returned within half an hour. Security were aware that Simmerby was under arrest and they had made sure that he was not out of their sight for one second. Simmerby handed Sir George a file marked 'Top Secret'. "You will disregard any previous orders and remain with security until I call for you. Security, take him out and keep your eyes on him until I require you to bring him back." As the door closed behind them, he opened the 'Top Secret' file. As he read page after page with increased intensity, the shock on Sir George's face became more apparent. "What is it Sir?" He was slow to respond but eventually he stared at Freddy and he was visibly shaken, "These orders are all apparently signed by me. The signatures on first view are mine but that cannot be as I didn't write any of this stuff and I certainly did not order Huntley Haverstock to be illiminated." Freddy stared back, the shock on their faces showed a dawning realisation that, yet again, their department had been infiltrated by a third party. "This needs a full investigation, I'll get Simmerby back in again and I want you to fill in any points that I might leave out." Back in the office Simmerby was becoming decidedly more uncomfortable, "Sir, I don't understand, your orders were very specific and I carried them out with my team to the best that I could." "How did you come by these orders?" "From you sir." "Damn it man I issued no such orders and come to think of it, I haven't had occasion to contact your office for some time. I'll ask you again, how did you receive these orders?" "In the dispatch box from your office sir." "Who brought them to you?" "Well, that was the unusual thing sir, they came by a courier but as it was top secret we did not think it too strange." "Be more specific man, was he Government or contract?" "The only identification was on his black uniform in the form of a Raven. More than that I don't know sir but I ran a check on the signatures on the orders and they all checked out." "Very well Simmerby that will be all for the moment but I want you and your team to stand down completely until I personally contact you again. Do you understand?" "Yes sir." "Simmerby, I want all of your available agents to investigate who this courier was and who he was working for and I want to be informed at all stages. You have jeopardized and embarrassed this office. You have murdered and threatened innocent people and harassed my personal team and until I get to the bottom of this your team have your direct orders to find that courier and you are suspended from all other activities until we catch this man. You and your office will keep me fully informed, daily and Iwill not tollerate any delay in any information reaching me, is that clear?" Simmerby left with the security gurds. "Well, Huntley, I think that we have been here before. They have used our own people to do their dirty work for them and , at least, your friend Lol will be able to come and go as he pleases now. I trust that you will let him knowthat the heat is off him?" "Of course I will sir, he will be most relieved." "You are back on full operations from now so stay in London and make this your headquarters for the duration. Do you still have the box?" "I have access to it at any time sir, it is safe and will remain so I can assure you sir." "Everything seems to revolve around that thing. It has all of our boffins totally foxed but if we knew its' properties then it might help us to understand what is so important about it. Will you let me have it? We need to find out something that will help." "It is getting late sir, I will bring it first thing in the morning." "Thank you, Huntley." Freddy left the office and headed for his apartment on the Embankment. He was looking forward to a bit of peaceful rest, for a change.

Chapter 13

The following day Huntley had the box ready to take into the office. He had not seen any news in the media or on television for some time so he turned on his television while he had his breakfast. He placed the box beside the TV so that he would be certain not to forget it. He went to make his morning coffee and returned to watch the latest news but as he watched the TV, the box caught his eye, it was changing shape and size. Tentatively Huntley touched the box but there was nothing to indicate that anything was happening, no vibration, no heat and no sound. He picked up the box and the box stopped any change or process that he had watched. To his amazement it was no longer a box and it would certainly no longer fit into his pocket. It was the shape and size of a rugby ball. He shook it and he heard the same rattle that he had heard before. Huntley found a shopping bag and popped the ball into it. He needed to get this thing to Sir George as soon as possible so he left for the office.

Sir George was amazed by the changes to the box and questioned Huntley about the circumstances but it confounded them both. One advantage now was that with a little disguise the box was unrecognisable to any prospective usurper. The news came that a new message had been received by Simmer by's office and the courier had been detained. "Well bring the courier here. We need to question him. I cannot believe these people, you even have to wipe their noses for them. Whatever happened to initiative?" The courier arrived under guard and was ushered to the vacant interview room. Sir George left him there to increase pressure on him before he and Huntley entered the room to interview him. Sir George led the questioning but had instructed Huntley to intervene if required. "What is your name?" "Billings" came the reply. "For whom do you work?" "Raven couriers." "Who sent this message?" Sir George had not even opened the envelope to see what it contained. "It came by wire from abroad." "Where from man?" "It came via Paris, from Geneva and from a Mr Zeute." "Do you know who this man is?" "No, we just deliver the messages that we are given."

Huntley looked at Sir George and indicated that he needed to speak to him in private and they both left the room. Huntley reminded him of the Geneva connection that he and Lol has looked into. "I don't believe that this billings chap has any information to give us but the company might know more. Shall I check them out with a visit?" "Yes, and I will see if I can get a trace on the origin of this message. I will just follow up on our Billings man just in case." Huntley got the Raven couriers address and headed over to their office. Sir George had read the message and informed Huntley that it contained his own signature, on immediate inspection and the instructions contained were even more insistent on Simmerby getting hold of the box to await further instructions. Huntley arrived at Raven's couriers and met up with the owner, Jed Bates. Jed was very co-operative and gave all the details he had on the sender of the messages. He had no details of the Geneva office other than the stamp "Geneva" but he knew the Paris office well and arranged a call. Jed spoke to Paris and obtained a P.O. Box in Geneva." "I am sorry that we can't be more specific but there is no way that we can source the P.O. Box." "You have been a great help, thank you, I appreciate all of your efforts."

Huntley left and returned to the office and confirmed that Billings knew nothing of interest in this case and they released him to return to Raven Couriers. In the mean-time Sir George had instructed Simmerby to reply to the message to confirm that he had the box in his possession but to delay for four days. This would give Huntley time to visit Geneva, obtain any information and, hopefully, be there when there was a pick up at the P.O. Box. The journey was uneventful but while he was there Huntley just had to do some shopping at Stanley's of Geneva. He also had to visit Krane's Seneca shop. Fashions were changing quickly in the sixties and while Huntley was not a particular follow of fashion he liked to keep up with the trends when he could. For his own shopping he went to Auburn Pants Factory Store and bought a few things for himself. The time came to get down to business so he headed for the Favette Postal Centre on Ovid Street. He needs to familiarise himself with the area before the courier or whoever was planning on picking up the message from London.

He identified the actual P.O. Box and checked the surrounding streets and then waited. It was late afternoon of the fifth day that a young boy picked up the message from the counter clerk. Huntley shadowed the boy while in the line at the counter and heard the boy say that it needed to be posted on to London. He wasn't able to hear the box number and he immediately discounted any involvement by the boy, obviously he was just a messenger. The post office was reluctant to divulge any information on the box number but after much negotiation and explanation of his mission they gave him what he wanted. He set off for London without delay. He was shocked as he travelled and considered the number, that in fact it sounded very much like a diplomatic box number. It was confirmed later that it was a diplomatic box but it had been de-commissioned years ago but by whom, no one knew and there was no record in file. It was cited in the old building quadrangle which meant if an observation point was to be set up it would have to be inside the building. Huntley arranged discrete access to the old building and chose an office directly opposite the old P.O. Box. As he sat in the window, he turned to look at the empty office, it looked as if everyone had just got up and left it as it was. Pens were still on the desk, an empty tea cup next to a loaded type writer and a file on safety open on a desk. He chuckled at the thought of the Marie Celest office. Dust covered everything and his gaze settled on his own footprints on the floor when he spotted a movement in the quadrangle. A post office worker approached and dropped the re-directed message into the P.O. Box. Huntley had a skeleton key and could have checked the contents of the box but chose not to as it might risk his cover. He decided to wait and see who would come to collect it and open the box. Time hung heavily as he waited and waited. The day passed into evening and then twilight and as darkness approached Huntley decided that the time to pounce on anyone collecting had passed but he waited again until dawn was imminent. 'Enough' he thought and risking it he headed for the box to check the message. He quickly left the office before it got light and went into the quadrangle and he opened the box with the special key to find that the box was completely empty. 'How could he have missed anyone opening the box, it wasn't possible?' he thought. 'I haven't missed anyone but how is the box empty?' He looked now at any possibility of accessing the box. He checked the wall but there was no sign of any break or lack of solidity. He checked the bottom of the box for any crevices that might conceal the message. Locking the box again he realised how tired he was so he headed for his flat to get some necessary sleep. Almost immediately after falling asleep, it seemed, the telephone rang. It was daylight and Sir George was calling him, "Come to the office immediately!" The phone went dead. Huntley got out of bed and washed and dressed and was in the office within the hour.

On arrival Simmerby was sitting opposite Sir George, "At last Huntley, come in and sit down. Simmerby here has another message with my name on it with instructions to deliver the box to the Ministry Mailing office. Did you see who it was who collected the message from Geneva?" Huntley just shook his head thinking it better not to give any report until Simmerby was out of the way. There was a delay but Sir George got the feeling that Huntley was not happy giving any information infront of outsiders so Simmerby was dismissed with instructions to return to the office at 3-o-clock in the afternoon. As soon as it was clear Huntley reported on his experiences. "No one came to pick up the message, No one! The box was empty but no one collected it! And how did Simmerby get hold of it? I sat in that dusty office nearly all night and saw no one after the postman delivered it. Wait, what am I thinking of? That office was filthy from years of neglect but the bottom of the P.O. Box was as clean as a whistle. No dust, leaves or rubbish of any sort. It has been accessed and used regularly and the only way that could happen without being seen is from the inside of the building but how?" Sir George picked up the phone, "I will get the plans of the old building sent up straight away, meanwhile I need to find who is getting hold of my stationery and who signs my signature. This is a very dangerous matter which has potential to breach all office communications with disastrous consequences. I'll get the plans to you as soon as I can, you go and take a break after your night vigil. You look shattered."

 Huntley made his excuses and left the office and headed for the downstairs restaurant for his breakfast below his flat on the Embankment. Mario's coffee would surely wake him up a bit. He realised that he hadn't had a decent meal for days. He ordered and enjoyed his Fusilli Gratinati washed down with a large glass of of Chianti followed by a large cup of Italian coffee. He was glad to have break from the investigation even for a few hours and leave Sir George to get on with things himself. This was a very complicated investigation and nothing made any sense. What was happening, how were things happening, who was behind it all and why was the box so important? He thought that the best plan was to find out how that P.O. Box was accessed so secretly. If he found the access point, it might give a clue as to who was involved. He slowly relaxed as he sipped his coffee but his attention was quickly diverted as he heard his name being mentioned to Mario. He looked up to see a very attractive brunette making her way to his table.

"Do you mind if I join you Huntley? I have file for you from records." She sat down before Huntley could say a word. "You have me at an advantage as I do not know your name." "I'm sorry, I should have introduced myself, my name is Judy Blain from the office of records. I was told to give this file in person." "How did you find me here?" "I was told by Sir George that I would most likely find you eating in this cafe." Judy passed the file across the table and Huntley looked hard at her. He was somewhat concerned by this approach and the fact that she was still sitting at the table, as if she was waiting for something. He considered his options but as he did so, she ordered an expresso. "Shouldn't you be getting back?" "I am on my lunch break now so I thought that I would combine the two things and have something to eat here. What would you recommend?" She ordered Maccheroni Al Quatro Formaggi on Huntley's advice and they both ate with very little conversation. Judy did not eat all of the generous portion of the meal and she quite suddenly got up and said, "We will have to do this sometime again, it was very nice meeting you." She fidgeted with her handbag and left.

CHAPTER 14

Huntley did not know what to make of this surprising encounter, was Sir George playing cupid? No never, it wasn't in his character but why would he send her and not page him as agreed? He felt that Judy had not been totally honest with him but he could see no reason, in retrospect, to be concerned. Huntley opened the file to find the plans of the old building adjacent to the quadrangle. The P.O. Boxes backed onto the old post room from where the post was sorted and delivered to the various departments and offices. That would explain how someone could access the boxes unseen and with frequent and recent use would also explain the dust free bottom of the box. Someone was accessing from inside of the old building and Huntley had to get into the place to see what the setup was and possibly gain some clues as to who it was going in and out of there without someone else knowing. He would get the keys and go this afternoon. He looked again at the plan and noticed that the old building was adjacent to offices still in use. These offices were separated by a corridor but it was clear from the plan that the corridor had been blocked and that the passage was not in use or accessible, at least at first glance. It had been blocked off years ago. It never ceased to amaze Huntley that such resources could be mothballed without any obvious reason or even discussion with other staff. This disused area must be worth a fortune in real estate and it was standing empty. He shrugged and thought it was no use to reason why he just had to get in there and find out for himself. Later Huntley was back at his vantage point in the old quadrangle but this time armed with keys to access the whole building. He unlocked the door next to the P.O. Box and went into a corridor. As he walked, he looked back to the entrance to see that the only evidence of any traffic in there was his own footprints. As he went from corridor to corridor, they were all the same with dust undisturbed for ages, no sign of anyone being here at all. Eventually he found the post room. The door swung open and Huntley hesitated to look at the floor. Behind the boxes and at the other side of the room the floor was covered by footprints but none from the door on this side of the room. The prints led to a door on the other side of the room but the plans did not show any door other than the one that he had used. The corridor separating the old building from the new was behind that wall and no access was shown from that corridor Huntley tried the door but the handle did not give and there was no sign of a lock on this side. It was obviously secured on the other side in the corridor.

He quickly left the post room making sure that it was locked and headed for the new building to look for access from that side. He could not remember who occupied that department of the ministry and as he aproached he could see the plaque read 'Ministry of Overseas Development'. Huntley thought that he could not risk searching the building whilst it was occupied so he planned to come back with the security officers later that evening. Out of curiosity, he telephoned records to talk to Judy Blain but they said that there was no one of that name in that department. Huntley called Sir George to inform him of events and the mysterious Judy Blain but on hearing that anme he told Huntley that he knew of her in the Ministry of Overseas Development. "It looks as if you are on the right track. I am going to be with you this evening when you do the search, I have a vested interest in this caper." Huntley was taken by surprise, Sir George very rarely got involved in the fieldwork after the Cuban affair.

Sir George was obviously very rattled by this case. Sir George arranged the search for eight pm. The autumn had the chill of winter as they entered the Overseas ministry accompanied by two-armed security guards. The Concierge at the desk confirmed that the building was empty and that Judy Balin had a ground floor office. He led the way to her office but told them that there was no corridor at that side of the building. Blain's office had a definite feminine touch, fresh flowers on her desk beside her name plate and on the bureau. The curtains were patterned with a delicate flower design. The office lacked windows but was well lit when they switched on the lights. The desk was tidy and the 'In Tray' was empty and the 'Out Tray' contained just one file. Against the wall where the corridor should have been was a beautiful antique book case filled with an astonishing variety of topics. Huntley picked up the file in the out tray and opened it to find him looking at himself. It was a large photograph taken in an Italian restaurant with a nice bottle of Chianti in the foreground. He had been totally unaware of being photographed and obviously it had been taken recently. Then he remembered Judy fiddling with her handbag earlier in the day, obvious really. 'So that was the purpose of their meeting today.' he thought. It hadn't been Sir George who sent her so it had to be the person who was pretending to be him but who was it? Yet again, whoever it was, knew of the plans made in Sir George's office but how? Freddy continued reading the file and the full report of the meeting in the restaurant. He searched the file for any clue as to who the report was made for but there were no names or references to any individual. Huntley replaced the file into the tray and took out the building plan to show Sir George where the corridor should be and the concierge confirmed that the wall behind the bookcase was where the corridor should be. They inspected the wall but could not find any door or breaks where there could be access. Huntley walked to the bookcase and tripped over the luxurious mat that was in front of it. He did not want to leave any trace of their visit so he bent down to straighten the mat but as he did, he noticed, where it was dislodged, tread marks underneath. He pulled the mat away from the bookcase to reveal tracks caused by the movement of the bookcase itself. He was about to ask for help in moving it but as he put pressure on it, it moved very easily to expose a hidden door behind. The door was not locked and opened smoothly into the corridor. As they entered the darkness of the corridor the security guards lit their bright torches to reveal a trail of footprints that led to a barred door. Huntley raised the bar to open the door to the old post room. It came as no surprise and now they knew how and who had collected the messages but who were they intended for? They carefully made sure that no trace of their visit was visible and they left the building binding the concierge to complete silence and secrecy. Sir George warned of the serious consequences if the concierge broke his promise. Back in the office Sir George set a twenty-four-hour watch on Judy Blain's activities and monitoring of telephone calls and communications to her office. They now had to wait for results but in the mean- time a full history report on Judy Balin was set in motion. The one thing that puzzled Huntley was why Judy had lied about being in the records department. She must have known that her lie would be found out so he decided to call on her first thing in the morning under the pretext of seeing her again. The next day bright and early Huntley luxuriated over an Italian breakfast before going to see Judy but was interrupted when Mario called him to the telephone. It was Sir George, "Miss Balin is on the move and in some sort of panic. You will not be able to intercept her as she has already shaken off our team at the airport. From air traffic control she appears to be heading for Ireland. We have alerted our agents over there and her flight is being monitored. I will see you when you get into the office." The phone went dead and Huntley went back to his breakfast that had been kept warm by Mario. "More trouble with the ladies boss?" asked Mario. "You don't know how right you are Mario." Huntley headed for the office after finishing his meal but decided to check the box that seemed to be at the heart of this matter. There seemed to be a definite atmosphere when he got to the laboratory. People were reluctant to communicate with Huntley so he headed straight to the senior official. "What has gone on here?" demanded Huntley. "Are Huntley!" said Professor Murton, "We did not expect to see you." "Obviously not but I want to see the work report on my box and I would like to see it now." "Well, that might not be possible." said Murton. "Why not?" "We are still working on it." "Well, I want to see your work and I want to see the box and I will not take no for an answer." "But...." "No buts, lead on now!" "I don't know if I am authorised to let you." "Stop now, lead on." The professor was reluctant but he knew that Huntley had the backing of Sir George so he led him to the central court yard.

The sight before him left Huntley speech-less. The huge shiny object before him was still the shape of a rugby ball but hundreds of times bigger. It was the size of a London, double decker bus. They both stood for what seemed ages before Huntley asked what had happened but the professor had no explanation. "How did it get out here?" "It was left in the safe cupboard over there in the central courtyard." "I don't see any cupboard!" "No, the cupboard has been totally destroyed. That pile of rubbish is what is left of it." No matter how Huntley pressured the professor it was clear that he had no answer that he could give. "Show me where the cupboard was." Huntley was led to the spot where the cupboard base was still bolted into the ground. "I must get on," said Murton "You know your way out." The professor headed back the way that they had come and Huntley was relieved to see the back of Murton. There was something about him that made Huntley feel uncomfortable. He looked around the yard but the only other thing in that space was the back-up generator. He spent some time looking at the massive box that at one time fitted into his pocket but there did not seem any explanation to the growth of it. He headed back to the office and wondered, on the way, about his reception at the lab. And he concluded that it must be down to guilt or failure to discover anything about the box. Their lack of providing any answers must have been very embarrassing. Sir George was astounded by Huntley's report and he was not alone at being mystified by the changes to the box. The fact that such an originally small object could grow to such an extent, was beyond comprehension. News had arrived about the activities of Judy Blain. She had headed for Wexford in southern Ireland and booked into the Ferrycarrig Hotel.

Huntley had been there many years before and had been impressed by the service and quality of his stay. The hotel overlooked a beautiful lake and the rooms and entertainment had been first class. The sense of isolation whilst at the hotel, sitting with a good quality glass of wine, looking out over the deserted lake was excellent. Whilst sitting and relaxing by the lake there were no buildings, houses or roads to break the vista of the tree lined lake. The fishing boats and pleasure boats gently rose and fell to the wind created gentle swell of the water. He fondly remembered his visit and the feeling of total relaxation that he felt there. He looked forward to following Judy there in the near future but his hopes were dashed when Sir George insisted that he would leave it to the Irish group to sort. Huntley did his best to argue his case for going but he could not get him to change his decision. It did, however, give Huntley time to go back to the lab. And take another look at that box, if that is what it could be called now. His London flat overlooked the river Thames and was only a few hundred yards from the Palace of Westminster bridge. He always enjoyed sitting in the restaurant below his flat at Mario's enjoying fine food and wine. He was sitting at his favourite table in Mario's as Mario approached him. "What is your speciality today, Mario?" "Good to see you Huntley, we are doing 'Gnocchi al Forno' today." "Ah, baked potato dumplings with stringy Mozzarella cheese, one of my favourites but you look very down today, Mario, what troubles you?" "We have had a compulsory notice to quit the building, if you haven't had your letter about your flat, then you will get one soon. They are going to knock down this whole block and extend the Westminster building." "Never!" exclaimed Huntley, "that is pure vandalism. I wonder who dreamed up that plan?" "It seems that they are going to make this a new entrance to the Houses of Parliament for security reasons." explained Mario. "We have only two months to relocate and there is little that we can do but to celebrate our friendly and your patronage, I will join you for a glass or two of my finest Barbera D'Asti, a fruity, soft red wine. I will go and retrieve a bottle or two to drown our woes." Mario came back to join Huntley as Mario's niece served them both their meals. "This is such a pleasure Mario, I am really going to miss being here. We have been friends now for a long time but I hope that we will be able to keep in touch when the time comes to leave." "We will drown our sorrows in style Mr. Huntley and look to a happy future." They savoured the wine when the lights suddenly went out. Mario struck a match and lit the table candles. "I will go and check what has happened to the lighting. After a few minutes the lights came back on and Mario returned. There was no explanation as to why the lighting had failed but the electric system had been compromised so Mario had turned off all but the electricity not used for cooking. They sat in the silence of the restaurant and peacefully enjoyed their repast. Later that evening when Huntley returned to his flat, he had a flash of inspiration. Mario had said that the electric system had been compromised and Huntley remembered the box growing when it was near his television. He wondered if there was a direct connection to the growth experienced when placed by the generator in the professor's yard. Maybe that was how the changes came about. The magnetic field created by the TV and the generator may be the reason for the changes.

Huntley hardly slept through the night and was up bright and early the next morning. He called at the ministry store and booked out a hand generator and almost ran to the laboratory. He insisted that he aws alone with the box and made sure that no one could observe his activities. He switched on the generator and held it close to the silver shape, his heart pounding in expectation. Nothing happened so he held the generator as close as possible and the shape responded. He backed away and the shape stopped changing. He tried the experiment again with the same result. The generator had a very low magnetic field but even that had the desired effect. He had to get a more powerful magnetic field to be absolutely certain. He left without any explanation to the 'Boffins' only to return from the equipment store with a far more powerful generator and the security team that had been present previously. The team stood guard to ensure that no one from the laboratory could see what was going on. Huntley stood in front of the box wondering how to proceed for the most positive results. He had concluded that the magnetic field created the changes but how to control those changes and possibly reverse them? He approached the box with the strongest magnetic field that he could create. As he got closer the box grew but as he almost touched the box a small hole appeared and it continued to grow as he held the field generator close. For the first time Huntley could see inside the box.

He noticed as he stepped away from the box that while the hole grew, the box didn't. He could see inside the box through the hole what had caused the rattle. It was now very small in comparison to the box but it lay in the bottom of the shape. It was pyramid in shape and looked to be of the same material as the box but it had to have different characteristics somehow. Why was it inside of the box? Was it just to see if it could be put inside or did it have some purpose? He stepped closer to the box to get a better view but he forgot that the field was still active and as he got level with the opening, it quickly closed. He had made contact with the surface of the box. The box, itself, reduced in size and made Huntley step back in surprise and all movement ceased. Was the box playing games with him? Reluctant to make any more mistakes Huntley decided to risk touching the box again with the magnet on its' surface and the reduction was immediate. As long as he was in contact with the box with the magnet it continued to reduce in size. He switched off the magnet when the box reduced to its' original size and put the box in his pocket. Taking the security team with him, he left the labs. and instructed the team to return all the equipment to the store.

Huntley went to see Sir George but he was out of the office, so Huntley poured a whisky and sank into one of the comfortable arm chairs in the suite room. He felt that he needed to calm his nerves after his experiences with the box and felt it in his pocket just to make sure that he had not been dreaming it all. He was determined to keep the information away from the 'Boffins', it seems that in the past their type had caused all the aggravation and death involved with the box. He knew that it would cause problems when they discovered that the box had gone but what Huntley had experienced was in the realms of science fiction. Huntley became more relaxed after his third large whisky and Sir George returned as He filled his glass and a large glass for Sir George. "I suggest that you take a seat sir and get a tight hold on your glass, you will be needing a drink when I finish telling you my discoveries." Huntley carefully and slowly told of the happenings and watched the jaw of his companion drop as he listened. When Huntley had finished his story Sir George drained his glass in one swallow. They both sat in silence, thoughts racing through their minds. The implications were devastating and frightening even though the full mystery of the box were still to be investigated. After a few more drinks and careful thought, Sir George broke the silence, "The Irish group have arrested Judy and her contact at the Ferrycarrig hotel and it looks as if we have the mastermind behind all of this in custody at last. It appears that the man in custody is Reuben King the grandson of the cousin and assistant of Albert King when Albert discovered the metal and created the box that came into your possession. Saville D. King was head of security here until a few years ago. He still had security clearance and he also had access to all offices in our department which means he had access to my stationery and signed documents that I had signed and cleared in the past. That explains how he could copy and impersonate my instructions to people in a variety of departments who had little to do with me on a daily basis. He had come across the experiments conducted on metals undertaken by Albert Reuben and we now know why he was prepared to kill to get his hands on the box. In the commercial market the knowledge of the box and how it could be used would be worth billions and billions of pounds.

I have no alternative now but to talk to the prime minister about this case, I just can't keep it to ourselves anymore." Huntley was shocked, "I am not sure that it would be wise to involve anybody else with this information yet. We do not know enough about the box to let anyone else know of its' existence. The properties will have military uses and miniature weapons could be smuggled into a country without anyone being the wiser. Who can we trust with this? We just can't make it public yet. Give me more time to get to know the box better and then we can discuss its' future. One Saville D. King is enough without creating another one, we might be the first on the list to be got rid of." "Do you know, you are right in what you say Huntley. Duty in this case is not the priority we will hold off for now and decide when we have more concrete evidence." "Thank you, sir, I really don't think that we can involve anyone and I mean anyone in this and particularly the 'Boffins' who are going to cause a great flap when they ask about the box. It would be funny if it wasn't so serious, I would love to see their faces when they look for a massive metal ball and find it gone." Sir George reassured Huntley, "I will deal with them when that happens."

Chapter 15

Huntley took the box from his pocket and a magnet from his other pocket, "Let's see what happens." He applied the magnet directly to the surface of the box and the side opened completely. Huntley could see the small pyramid inside and without thinking he tipped it out into his hand. It was smooth and cool and on inspection he could see some markings on the side. "Have you a magnifying glass sir?" He was handed a large glass from the desk and looked carefully at some writing on one side and some symbols on the others. On the base of the 'right' pyramid was a complex formula. "We will need a Metallurgical chemist to decode this if we are to understand it but who could we trust to do it?" "What are the symbols?" asked Sir George. "One is a set of concentric circles and there is another set with a cross through it. The third one looks like a screw." As they studied the symbols the phone rang. It was the priority phone and Sir George answered immediately. He listened for some time before replacing the receiver. "That was a report from Ireland, Saville and Judy had been arrested on suspicion of murder amongst other charges and Saville had made a request for his statuary phone call. When they came back to check on them, they were both dead. The medics confirmed death by potassium cyanide." "Well, we can't bring them to justice now and hopefully that closes the case but why request a phone call if you plan suicide?" asked Huntley. It was a question that they were both puzzled by but it occurred to them both that there may be someone else that had been contacted and involved. It might not be over after all. They would have to wait and see what developed.

They returned to the box and the pyramid. Hours went by unnoticed but they had more and more information on the properties of the box and they astounded by the strength and abilities that they discovered. Neither had noticed the time and it was late in the evening so they decided to call it a day. Huntley kept the box in his possession and Sir George did not raise any objection in fact he thought it the best thing to do. If there was someone else involved his office may not be as secure as it might be. Before parting they agreed that they would consider the case closed even thought there was a possible doubt of some other person being involved but the priority was to agree what to do with the box. Back at his flat Huntley kept the box with him at all times, he didn't even trust it to his safe. Earlier he had discovered how to control the box, open it, close it and stop any growth or change. He had also learned how to control the shape and had now made it flat based and resembling a paper weight. He had taken a label from a bought item and stuck it on the base of the box.

Huntley slept well that night and rose refreshed in the morning and quickly showered and dressed. He headed for breakfast in Mario's and realised that he had no plans for the day and, in fact, not for tomorrow either. He pondered on the fact that he had been so pre-occupied with events that he had lost touch with all friends and relations and he was now without any close family. Mario had his problems as he sat down with Huntley who was conscious of the problems that Mario faced. They talked over their coffees and did their best to put the world at rights. Mario told Huntley that the restaurant was closing early today and all of his family were coming together for a party to celebrate the happy years spent in the business. They were also going to plan the future by gathering ideas and considering possibilities Huntley was invited. He was really happy to be invited and looked forward to meeting the family again, most of whom he knew. He thanked Mario and set off for a shopping spree in the city.

As he walked down Oxford Street he came to a gents' outfitters and in their window was a pin stripe Italian suit. It looked the business so he went in and found that it was a perfect fit straight off the peg. He kept the suit on and carried his other clothes in the bag provided by the shop. He had never paid more than thirty pounds for a suit but this one was worth every penny of the forty-five pounds that he paid for it. Huntley wandered around the city feeling free and relaxed than he had felt for a long time, was the case really closed? He dismissed the thought of the box and concentrated on strolling around without feeling any pressures. He walked and walked in the spring sunshine passing through Leicester Square, Picadilly, Nelson's Column, Horse Guards Parade and finally arriving in St. James Park walking on to Westminster Abbey. It was late afternoon when he finally arrived back at his appartement. He showered and changed into casual clothing before heading downstairs to meet up with Mario. It was strange to see the pavement outside of the cafe without a member of staff encouraging passers-by to partake of the restaurant foods and drinks. The pavement tables had gone and the windows were covered by curtains that had recently been put up as if to shut out the outside world. Other than the restaurant sign gave away that it was not a quiet nineteenth century residential building. The embankment was quiet but the traffic still crossed over Westminster bridge. The lowering sun cast shadows, moving and shimmering on the Embankment and the river Thames. Few boats were moving on the river but a pleasure boat full of revellers was passing by. They were probably heading for Kew Gardens or even up to Hampton Court Palace. He turned and headed for the door of the restaurant but as he approached the door opened to reveal a smiling Mario who gave him a warm welcome. "We are all here and Gino was watching for you to arrive. Let me introduce you to all of our family. You know more of them, the boys of course you know but I don't think that you have met my wife Bella and my daughter Gina. They are very rarely at the restaurant."

Huntley shook hands with Bella but when he turned to meet Gina he was stunned by her beauty and his assured manner lost some of its' control. For an Italian girl she was very pale skinned and she had blond hair. She was in her early twenties and when she saw the effect that she had on Huntley, she smiled an embarrassed smile. Mario and Bella exchanged a knowing look and Mario dragged Huntley away to meet his brother and his wife who did most of the restaurant meals. Huntley expressed his appreciation for their culinary skills and he was soundly hugged by Mario's brother. Mario poured the drinks and the music and chatter soon filled the room with happy sounds. In the melee Gina and Huntley slowly gravitated together. Their eyes had met on a number of occasions throughout the evening and they gazed longer as the evening went on. Finally, they met and spent the rest of the evening in each-others company until all awkwardness had gone and they relaxed and enjoyed the rest of the night. They promised to meet the next day and the next day became the next and the next. They were very happy together and the fun became romance but their time together was cut short one morning by a call from Sir George, "Huntley I need you in my office immediately. Whatever you are doing drop it and get here as fast as you can! What I have for you is very important and urgent." Huntley contacted Gina and explained. They agreed to meet as soon as they were both free.

Chapter 16

The scene as Huntley arrived at the office took him by surprise, the room was full of people. Senior Government officials, security officers and Sir George who looked most uncomfortable. He was sitting at his own desk but on the wrong side, his usual seat was occupied by a most unpleasant looking little man who addressed Huntley as he entered, "Ah, Haverstock, do come in and sit down." The only seat available was beside Sir George who avoided eye contact with him as he took his seat. "Now Haverstock, I believe that you have something that belongs to us. Your appartement is being searched as we speak but my team have not found the box, you will tell me where it is." "I do not believe that we have met before and as you have failed to introduce yourself I think not." "Do not get smart with me!" exploded the little man as he leaped out of Sir George's chair. A large man stepped forward and said, "Maybe I can help to explain things here, I am the Right

Hon. James Honeysuckle M.P. Minister for Defence, Research and Development. The gentlemen here are the internal Westminster security team and Mr. Smeaton here is conducting and heading the investigation into the whereabouts of a certain object. Please continue Mr Smeaton and be more civil in your questioning." Huntley watched Smeaton deflate at the admonition from the M.P. and he looked around at the stern faces of the security team most of whom were trying to avoid a smile. He caught a glance from Sir George who gave a look of caution to Huntley. Huntley acknowledged the warning. "Well, Mr. Haverstock?" Huntley replied, "What is it that you believe that I have that belongs to you?" "You came across a small metal box some time ago and Sir George has confirmed that it is your possession." "Ah that thing, yes, I am afraid that I do not know of its' whereabouts it was misplaced or dropped somewhere and I have looked for it but I have been unable to find it again. It was as you say just a small box of no real significance and of very little value." There was a charged silence in the room and Smeaton looked as if he was about to explode but Honeysuckle stepped in again, "The box is of great value to us and was developed through government research and development jurisdiction in the north of England. It is something that we dealt with years ago and a 'D' notice was applied to maintain secrecy. It was never to be let out of the top-secret unit ever. We do not know how you came to have it in your possession but I hope that you understand the gravity of the situation and give us your full co-operation."

Huntley considered his comments for a few moments, "I am quite concerned at the heavy-handed approach to getting any form of co-operation from us and the way in which you are treating us. Sir George and I are trusted and loyal servants of the Queen and Westminster and the government owe a great deal to the services provided by Sir George and his team. Your methods seem to deem us some sort of criminals but I have told you that the box has truly disappeared and without any pressure from your team I am sure that Sir George and I will give you all the support that we can." Huntley looked at Sir George who nodded his approval. "We will do all that we can to return what belongs to you." Smeaton thumped the desk with his fist and drew himself up to his most diminutive height but a raised hand from Honeysuckle pre-empted any outburst. "I believe that you are right Mr. Haverstock, how would you like to proceed with our discussion?" "Firstly, this security team is quite out of place and totally inappropriate and Mr. Smeaton is not helping to provide a congenial atmosphere for discussion. I am sure that in a more relaxed atmosphere we can make progress."

Huntley took a breath and looked around the office. Honeysuckle showed a fleeting sign of frustration but after a brief silence he waved Smeaton and his team out of the office. Huntley tilted his head to Sir George to retake his desk chair. As Sir George reclaimed his rightful position Honeysuckle and his two aides sat down facing him. "Thank you, Huntley. Would you gentlemen care for a drink? Tea, coffee or something stronger?" They all opted for something stronger. As they drank their choice of drink there was a feeling of relaxation not previously experienced. Honeysuckle broke the silence, "Well, I believe that you are both aware of the history of the box, particularly you Mr. Haverstock as your family members were on the team that developed it. How the box came to light again after it was classified and seccured we do not know but we know that somehow it came into your hands, Huntley but of course it is after all government property." Huntley was aware from the use of his name that Huneysuckle was trying to defuse the former pressure. Honeysuckle continued, "It is highly secret and must be handed over to the correct section for safe keeping." Sir George replied, "Huntley has told you that the box has disappeared and that he and I will do all that we can to retrieve it for you. Is that not correct Huntley?" "It is sir but I must ask why such an insignificant object is of such importance?"

Honeysuckle's frustration showed itself again but he took a deep breath, "The nature of the box is top secret and of national security so I am afraid that I cannot divulge any information to you or anyone else. I will have to insist that you find it and return it to me without delay." Huntley knew, probably, more about the box than Huneysuckle did but he said, "Very well, leave it with us and we do our very best to trace it for you, that is all that we can do."

The group opposite shuffled and whispered but eventually Huneysuckle and his aides stood and indicated that they were leaving, "As soon as possible Sir George and I will hold you personally responsible." At that they left the office. As the group left, they both sank into their chairs with great relief. "I need a refill." said Sir George, "and I am sure that you do too. You took one hell of a risk talking to them like that and they will be watching your every move, mine as well. They will be watching for you to go to collect the box where ever you have hidden it." "What the hell is going on? You are head of security, who were those clowns?" "No clowns Huntley, they are beyond security and they are very dangerous. It is a group that neither of us want to upset. It is the first time that I have had proof that they actually do exist, before this they were just a story from legend.

What have you done with the box?" "It is safe but I have no intentions of handing it over to them or anyone else until I get to know the score. You, know some of the box's characteristics but I have discovered a whole lot more. By the way, are we being monitored in here?" Huntley pointed to Sir George's desk. Sir George stared at his desk with a start and he pointed at a desktop lighter that was not belonging there. Sir George got up and waved Huntley to leave the room with him. He led the way to a secure interview room at the top of the building. "How did you know Huntley?" "I didn't recognise the lighter and I know that you don't smoke. Are you sure that these people are on our side? How can we check on them?" "That will be difficult Huntley. As I said these people are phantoms and not many even people know of their possible existence. I can tell you that Huneysuckle is genuine as an elected representative in charge of the Ministry for R and D. He has had to be checked again and again but the rest of them, I don't know. You said that you have found more out about the box?"

"Yes, sir but can I even tell you? Let me just say that with what I know I could invade any country in the world and they would know nothing about any invasion until it was too late to set up any defences." "What? You must be mistaken." Huntley shook his head, "No mistake sir, it is no wonder that they want to get hold of it and they obviously know some of its' capabilities. Anyone who has control of the box could hold the world to ransom. "Huntley go and get the box, we can't risk them finding it."

"Okay sir but we can't keep calling it 'The Box' let's call it 'Mary'." "Excellent! First to get you out of here without being seen and followed."

Chapter 17

Sir George led the way back to the office and into one of the guest suites, one that Huntley had not seen before or even knew existed. In the bathroom was a full-length mirror. At the touch of a hidden switch the mirror rotated and allowed them to access the passage behind. Along the passage was a lift door. Sir George entered the code and the lift door opened. At the same time the mirror closed. They descended in the lift and on opening they were on the underground rail system. Sir George explained that Sir Winston Churchill had used this very system during the second world war. It was now not used and many in government knew that it was there. Sir George led on along the rail track to another lift entrance. The lift ascended and to Huntley's surprise he was on the Embankment opposite Mario's restaurant. Huntley now knew how Sir George had frequently arrived to see him unobserved and unheralded. Huntley looked around and saw two men standing on the Embankment. We will have to come back later when it gets dark. The appartement is under surveillance and there is no way of getting past them unobserved.

They retraced their steps and went back to the office to return as soon as darkness fell. Back on the Embankment Sir George remained hidden in the lift entrance while Huntley crept unobserved in the dark to his doorway which was set back in the shadow from the street lighting. He quickly went to his flat and found it an absolute mess. The place had been thoroughly searched and not a lot of care had been taken in the process. Draws had been emptied on the floor, cupboard contents strewn around, the bed had been stripped but amongst all the mess the paperweight. 'Mary', was on the floor. He couldn't risk carrying it out in case he was seen and he thought for a while before he had a brain wave, mould to his chest shape and wear the thing like clothing.

Leaving the flat he reached the downstairs door and saw the two men opposite on the Embankment. He looked to see Sir George still in the lift doorway. Huntley hadn't realised that a lift was actually inside a police box. Huntley had seen police going in and out of the very same box on a number of occasions but had never really taken any notice of it. He waited for a while and as the two men turned to watch some movement on the river he headed for the police box. He had gone only a few yards when he heard a shout. He had been spotted so he ran as fast as possible and crashed into the police box and Sir George shut the door immediately. They descended in the lift. They both knew that they had been discovered but Sir George just smiled. The men pursuing them forced their way into the locked police box only to find an empty police box. Nothing at all unusual at all, stone floor, standard equipment but totally empty. Men appeared on the Embankment from all directions searching for Huntley. They had no idea how he had evaded their trap.

Back in the office they parted and went to their allocated quarters. Huntley couldn't sleep he was expecting visitors at any time. They must be furious at being outsmarted and he wondered what their next move would be. He reshaped 'Mary' and took the instruction key out to check for any more information. What else was written on it? He took the magnifying glass to look at the message on the base. It read: 'Never allow this to fall into the wrong hands, it is very dangerous!' Huntley wondered if it just meant what was written or did it have a specific meaning? On one side was written 'Texture by unlock magnetic contact' What does that mean, thought Huntley. He decided to try and sleep on it, so he put the key back inside 'Mary'.

He looked around the room that Sir George had given him. This was not a room that he had known of previously. There were a number of guest suites but this one was very grand. The building was very old and must have been a town house of some distinction years ago. The ceilings were very high and were decorated with plaster fruit and vines that looked as if they were hanging down ready to be eaten. There was a family crest painted and highlighted with gold leaf or gold paint. The walls were all oak panelled and the floor carpet was deep pile and very regal. There was everything needed for a pleasant stay, a four-poster bed, a bar, an en-suite bathroom and a writing desk. Relaxing on the four-poster bed Huntley slipped into a slumber and some disjointed and disturbing dreams, the box, messages everywhere, the key, memories of his grandfather and the tails that he used to tell him when he was a child. Images of the old house that they had lived in with his grandfather during his early years and images of the forbidden under stair cupboard. Being young and inquisitive he had peeped into the cupboard on one occasion and seen what looked like a shiny bomb.

Huntley woke with a start with the realisation that that was 'Mary' under the stairs all those years ago. He was surprised that it was light and he had slept through all the night. He heard in the distance the sound of a telephone ringing and the voice of Sir George answering. He got up and quickly washed and dressed. When he joined Sir George breakfast had been delivered and Sir George was eating and reading the newspapers. Huntley looked at the full breakfast available on the table, a nice way to start the day. "Well, you are in demand this morning, Huneysuckle was demanding to know of your whereabouts yesterday evening. I assured him that you did not leave this building last night or at any other time since we talked to him. He seemed to be reluctant to accept my story but I told him that we had been so concerned by the seriousness of the case that we had had a few too many drinks and that we had overslept to get over the indulgence." "That confirms that it was his men who were watching on the Embankment last night but I have more to tell you about 'Mary'." They finished eating in silence. "I had the office scoured for listening devices and four were found and disposed of. They left the building by the main entrance and walked along Whitehall towards Westminster bridge. They knew that they were not alone but they were well out of earshot and Huntley went over all that he had recently discovered about 'Mary'. The main message on the key was: 'Keep this out of the wrong hands' and not allow anyone in power to get control of it. It gave too much power to those who could corrupt that power. He told Sir George that it could be changed into any shape or size and disguised as something quite harmless but it could contain powerful and destructive contents. "It appears that my family members learned how dangerous it was and that this amazing material could be used to even destroy the world as we know it. They took great risks to protect the knowledge and keep it from anyone outside of their team but somehow their discoveries were leaked. I now realise why poor John was killed, he gave his life to protect the box and he passed on the responsibility to defend it to me. He has made me the custodian of the box and I have decided to keep the family tradition alive. I will be keeping the secret from everyone and I believe that you and I have the same responsibility to protect it.

    I Propose to let Honeysuckle know that one of his men found the box along with some other things that they took during their search. I will hide 'Mary' in a place that no one will ever find her."

Sir George sat and looked at Huntley. He said nothing and he was thinking hard about all that had happened. Eventually he agreed with the plan, "Do not even tell me what you plan to do with her. I will back you with Huneysuckle and we will head for your flat now and pretend to do a search. He will be aware that we have been there and that will lend credence to our story. There were so many of his men involved that they will be running around like headless chickens for a lifetime looking for the culprit. It also gets him off my back neatly. If we can get him to believe that one of his own men has lost it somehow, then it may hopefully conclude this matter forever. Leave things as they are for a few days and I will arrange another meeting with Honeysuckle. Let us both come up with a strategy for diverting attention away from us and onto his own group."

CHAPTER 18

Huntley's thoughts turned to Gina. He would take a day or two away from London on the pretext of further enquiries. He could easily lose any would be followers. When he got back to his flat, he went downstairs to visit the restaurant. Although the place was closed, he was sure that he could get a meal with Gina's family. He was still wearing 'Mary' like a closefitting vest and he was surprised how comfortable it had become. His knock on the door was answered by Gino who gave Huntley a typical Italian type hug in welcome. He was dragged upstairs to join the rest of the family. Gina was so pleased to see him again and hugged him as if it had been years since they had been apart. Huntley felt like a guest of honour as they sat down to eat. Gina told him that she was leaving for Italy the next morning to conclude some family business. Huntley quickly thought and said that he would be happy and honoured to escort her on her travels. He explained that he had a few days free and it would be great to see Italy and experience a little sunshine and warmth. The fact that he did not mention being with Gina did not pass unnoticed around the table and knowing looks were exchanged. Mario was delighted to agree to them going together and that Gina would not be alone. He went ot get a bottle of his finest to celebrate and wish them well on their journey together. They all toasted the couple and Huntley got the distinct impression that Mario could hear wedding bells already ringing out. The thought had also occurred to him as the evening went on with happy chatter, dancing to loud music and drink in steady supply.

Eventually everybody retired to their beds and the next morning Huntley booked the same flight to Italy and they were in the air and on the way to Italy before lunchtime. They landed at

Fiumicino Rome airport in the early afternoon. They were met by Francesca, Gino's cousin and driven to the town of Fiumicino to the family restaurant Il more on the Via Delle Carpe. The restaurant overlooked a sizeable lagoon and beyond that the Tyrrhenian-sea. Francesca and her family only spoke Italian, no English, so Huntley needed Gina to translate any conversations in which he was involved. The welcome was warm and friendly but that soon changed when Gina told the family how Huntley had joined her on this trip. The wine started to flow and Huntley was treated like the prodigal son and from there onwards Gina was chaperoned constantly by Francesca's aunt. They spent the evening visiting the famous sights of Rome but spent much of the time at spots in the city not visited by by tourists. Gina pointed out the fiscal centre where she was to transact her business dealings on the following day. They went to the Castel Saint Angelo bridge and took a river boat ride along the river Tiber. They sipped their drinks as they floated past the Palace of Justice and St. Peter's Basilica all under the watchful eye of their chaperone. Gina explained that she was to pick up a family treasure the next day and fly back to London in the afternoon.

The treasure was necessary for the future plans for all of the family. Gina was also to collect a present that was deposited for her, when she was very young, by her grandmother for the time when she reached a certain stage in her life. It was a small brush and comb in a shiny box. It was the next morning and they were at the building where the safety deposit box was opened by the bank representative and Gina collected all the contents. As they walked back Gina showed him the box and as she handed it to him a man ran straight at Huntley, it was Honeysuckle, shots rang out and bullets struck Huntley in the chest. He fell to the floor as if dead, assisted by the impact of the bullets. Huneysuckle grabbed the box and ran off. It all happened so quickly that Gina was stunned and she froze as she saw Huntley laid on his back on the ground. She was sure that he was dead. As she started to recover. Huntley drew a deep breath and got to his feet. Gina looked at the holes in his shirt and her mouth dropped open in surprise as Huntley smiled at her. "You should be dead" said Gina. "You are right but I took a few precautions just in case, Huntley smiled again knowing that 'Mary' had saved his life. He was still wearing it like a vest. His hand went to his chest and as he took it away, two flat bullets fell into his hand. He said nothing as he put the bullets into his pocket. Gina was full of questions and she was still shocked by the whole thing. Huntley explained that it was part of his job from time to time and such risks can sometimes happen. He told her that he had been fully prepared for just such an attack. It occurred to him that if 'Mary' had alerted the airport security screening he may not have been wearing it. That was another characteristic of 'Mary'. The metal involved was surprising him all the time.

    Huntley alerted the support team of events and a search party was sent to find Huneysuckle. Gina was very quiet on their journey back to London and Huntley felt that she was more shocked at events than she had shown. She was very moody as they travelled back to the Embankment and she did not invite him in. He went back to his flat but was very unhappy with the response from Gina and he hoped that it was not fatal for their relationship. He reported back to the office the next morning to be greeted by Sir George. "Good morning, Huntley. We thought that it was all over until that event in Rome but it appears not." "Any news on Huneysuckle sir?" Unfortunately, no, the Italian police lost him at the airport. He was spotted by our team entering the airport but from then on it was the Italian police who took over." "He is going to be a bit upset when he finds the contents of the box that he took. It was a hair set but he may believe that was how I disguised it, however that will not last long, he is sure to discover his mistake." "I ran a further check on his background and it seems that he is a metallurgical chemist and on checking his family there was a member of his family who had dealings with Albert Reuben. During the war his father was in the government scientific research and development team. He has misled our security for years and he has been trying to trace the box for as long as he can remember. I just wonder how many others there are who have some knowledge of its' existence?"

"Well, that confirms my decision. I am going to make sure that no one will ever get their hands on 'Mary'. No one can be trusted to use it for the good of mankind. It would appear that it just represents power and wealth. I am sorry but not even you will know what has happened to it." Sir George nodded his agreement. Huntley headed for the restaurant and was greeted by Gino who handed him a note and told him that Gina had left the country that morning. The family had also decided to relocate away from London and preparations were well underway to leave. Gino shook Huntley by the hand with tears in his eyes. The door closed and Huntley was stood outside reading the note. Gina had been truly shocked by events and felt the she could not spend her days with someone who faced such risks. She signed off with love but assured him that they would never meet again.

Huntley went into his appartement and headed for his bedroom but as he approached, he noticed the bedroom door was ajar. The light from the bedroom window showed a shadow of someone standing behind the door. It was a scenario that he had planned for when he first took the booking. He had placed a small mirror high up in the bedroom that gave a perfect view of the rear of the door. There, stood Honeysuckle with a gun ready for action.

Huntley went to his desk and took the power stun gun from the drawer. He approached the door and without hesitation fired at the door and the man standing behind it. The powerful stun lines passed through the thin panel on the door and struck its' target, Honeysuckle fell to the floor unconscious. Huntley secured his hands and feet and called the office. A team arrived with Sir George within minutes of his call. Huntley searched his pockets and found the small shiny box, Gina's present. He would later drop it at the restaurant so that at least she would get her grandmother's sentimental present.

Sir George congratulated Huntley on his capture but that changed nothing. Honeysuckle would face the full power of the law but there were others so nothing was resolved. Huntley was invited to join him to report to the Prime Minister and to a banquet later. The P.M. was assured that the box had been lost somewhere in all the happenings and that the information would be circulated to all departments who had any knowledge of it. Sir George received a commendation for his successful completion of the investigation and Huntley was also given recognition. They parted that evening and Huntley told Sir George that he was taking leave and would be Freddy Goodchild again for some time. Sir George said that he was deserving of some time to himself but assured him that while he was head of security his services would be required in the future.

The next day Huntley headed north not knowing what he would do but he was determined to keep his promise to Lol and book them both a long holiday on the company finances. He started looking forward to planning where they were going, probably touring to all the places that they had dreamt of as kids together at school. As he travelled up the M1 on his way home a small cage containing a small pyramid swung gently on his car keys. He was confident that no on knew where 'Mary' had finished up but in the Houses of Parliament the lobby was full of M.P.'s and visiting public walking past the statue of Winston Churchil. He seemed to have been cleaned and polished to a shiny brightness. On close inspection he also seemed to have a secret smile on his face.

CHAPTER 19

The street was dark, wet and windy as the girls walked home after the evening out at the youth club. "Well, this is where I leave you." said Wendy as she turned into her street. The response of goodnight came from Carolyn and Jane as they headed for their homes. "I don't like this dark road, you would think that the council had no funds for lighting, just two lamps for this whole road." Moaned Jane, "I agree, I always hate coming down here on my own in the dark." said Carolyn. The two girls plodded on battling against the wind and rain. Jane said her goodbyes as she turned for home, Carolyn had a few hundred yards before she arrived at her street but as she gathered her coat collar closer, she stumbled over something large and soft. In the dark she peered down at the lump in the pathway and horror caused an uncontrollable scream. Time seemed to stop and her scream seemed to go on and on but she almost fainted as a hand shook her shoulder. The lady from number 58 had heard her and run to see what had happened, she had not noticed the body on the floor and she thought that the girl was having a fit. "What is it?" and Carolyn pointed to the floor. Mrs Turner shone her torch in the direction of the body and stifled a gasp as she saw the bloodied corpse on the ground.

The police asked Carolyn what had happened but Carolyn could give no information other than how she had found the body. In the safety of her home, they were gathered in the kitchen, her mother calming Carolyn as best that she could. Mrs. Turner was there and she was no more able to give the police any information about events. The Inspector arrived at last after examining the body, "Thank you everyone for your help, we will leave you in peace now as you have all made a statement. I am sorry that you have had such a nasty experience." He gestured to the uniform officers to leave and as the last one left, he said "Please don't speak to anyone about what happened this evening." Back at the Police Station inspector Brown gathered his team for debrief and on completion he headed for the Chief Constables office.

"We have a delicate situation on our patch Sir. The body that was discovered this evening is the local MP and the paperwork that I found on him is Top Secret. He was brutally murdered, whoever did this made doubly sure that the MP could not survive the attack, it was a very professional murder. There is no evidence that there was a search of the body for information, they just confirmed that the hit was definite." The Chief Constable, who was standing,

slumped into his seat and stared at Inspector Brown. "Was it the local Conservative MP?" Brown nodded. "Can we keep this quiet and away from the press for the time being?" "Unless the families involved say anything I think we can keep it under wraps for the moment Sir but not for long, questions are bound to be asked. We will need to contact the secret services in Whitehall as the papers on him were from their records, they had their stamp all over them." "Who is in charge there?" "I understand that it is a Sir George Curswell Sir." "I will contact him straight away and I suppose that they will take over any investigations, so you can stand down for the moment. I will keep you informed of any developments Brown." "Very well Sir." Inspector Brown turned and left the room.

Sir George Curswell sat in his office looking through the paperwork found on the body of a member of Parliament. The information was Top Secret but was only information about service staff and their responsibilities in Sir Georges department. Why would an MP have such information on him and for what purpose? Sir George mused. Why would anyone want to kill but leave Top Secret information untouched? It made no sense to him but there had to be a pressing need to do something like this. As it was such a delicate situation, he considered his options and settled, after much thought, to activate Huntley Haverstock again. It had only been a few weeks since Huntley had been stepped down. Knowing him he would be bored on leave anyway, Sir George placed his regular advertisement to recall H. Haverstock.

Freddy Goodchild was having breakfast as the Daily Paper was stuffed through his letter box. Having opened the newspaper, the advertisement from Whitehall took him by surprise. It is only weeks since he was given leave. He packed after breakfast and set off to Whitehall.

CHAPTER 20

Freddy had arrived in Whitehall, now in his role of Huntley Haverstock, he was given all the information regarding the demise of the MP. "What I am puzzled by is the staff information held by this MP? Why would he be carrying it and where was he headed with it? What was his intention holding such important information and why put everyone here at risk? "I don't know Huntley, that is what you have to find out and why he was murdered in such a violent manner." replied Sir George. "Is all the information in this file on the MP?" "Affirmative."

Huntley headed off to his London apartment with all the paperwork including the papers with staff details. His previous accommodation had been bulldozed on the south bank of the Thames. He recalled the Italian family and their great food in the café where he rented the upper floor of the café. "Great days" he mused. He now lived in a Whitehall owned building with all modern fixtures and fittings but it did not hold a candle to the café.

The phone rang and Huntley answered, "Hello, is that Huntley Haverstock?" "Yes." Came the reply, "My name is Peter Curswell and I have been sent to assist you by Sir George and I wondered if I could meet up with you today?" "Course we can get together, I take it that you are related to the boss?" "Yes, we are brothers but I am younger and more attractive." "That wouldn't be too much of a surprise, where are you now?" "In Sir Georges' office." "Do you know the Toklas Café, just off Temple place?" "Yes, can we meet in about half an hour?" "Fine, I'll set off now and order some coffees for when you get there." "Okay."

Huntley set off for the café and he strolled along the Embankment to Temple Place in the warm sun, which was unusual in October, it was usually wet and cool but he felt a sense of wellbeing teamed up with Sir Georges brother. If he was as reliable and honest, as a team, they wouldn't go far wrong. He was beaten to the café by Peter and Huntley could not mistake the man waiting, it was a Sir George double. "I am pleased to meet you, Peter." As they shook hands. "Likewise, I am glad to meet up here, I just love the croissants that they do here." They sat at a window table and ordered coffee and croissants. "How much have you learned about the case Peter?" "All the information that was available I have studied but it is very strange that an MP was killed and the paperwork was still with him." "That is our starting point, it contained all the

names and occupations of people in our department but my details are not there because I was erased some time ago. I suppose Sir George told you all about it?" "Yes, I was given background on your career." "One thing that I noticed, Peter, about the paperwork was that it was a fax and that means that it was a copy and it must have been taken from office records in Whitehall." "Well spotted I didn't notice that." "It means that someone with access to the office is involved." Peter stared at Huntley." I don't know if my brother knew that?" Yet again there was the suspicion that there was someone passing information out of the department, which meant another leak in security, thought Huntley. It was late afternoon and as they enjoyed their coffee, an Evening Standard dealer set up his advertising board across the road and Huntley saw the headline on the board, 'Secret Investigator enlisted to find the murderer of MP.' "Look over there, Peter!" Peter stared at the headline in disbelief. "How could they possibly have that information and so quickly?" Huntley quickly set off for the Evening Standard offices. Peter was doing his best to keep up with him. Huntley changed his mind when he thought of 'Secret

Investigator' on the board, clever ploy or not he was not going to compromise his anonymity with this case. He halted abruptly, taking Peter by surprise. He explained why he had changed his mind and Peter understood immediately. "This is something else Peter, a possible clever plot by whoever is involved and quite astounding at the speed of reporting. We are up against something that I have not encountered before. We will have to think carefully before we take any action. Look, it's getting on, I will meet you tomorrow at Sir Georges' at 0830hrs, is that okay for you?" "Sure thing, have a nice evening Huntley." "That won't be as easy as I would like, see you tomorrow." He headed back to his apartment and called sir George. "Hello Sir, have you seen todays' Standard?" "No, is there something I should know?" "Yes Sir, there is a headline report on a secret investigator being brought in the find the murderer of an MP." "What? How? Who? what the hell is going on?" "I was going to find out where the Standard got their information but it might have compromised my identity. Can you find out where they got it?" "I can do more than that, I can slap a "D" notice on their publication." "Too late Sir, it is already in the public domain." "I will give their Editor something to think about. Leave it with me." "I will be in your office at 0830hrs in the morning if that's okay Sir?" "Right." Was the response as the phone went dead. Huntley poured himself a large whisky and sat down to order his mind. This situation has a number of possibilities, foreign spies, political plots, departmental investigations and so on. So many alternatives. His mind buzzed for hours but no answers were coming to the fore. He thought that he would sleep on it and maybe things would be a little clearer. After a couple more glasses he retired to a night of disturbed and broken sleep. The next morning in the office Sir George told Huntley and Peter of his conversation with the Editor of the

Standard. The Editor had not been very co-operative at first but the pressure had been applied and he eventually gave his source. "It appears that there is a news group that has leaped onto the scene that sells sensitive and sensational news items all over the place and it offers scoops at inflated prices for those who will pay for it. This was one of those occasions, only the Standard had this particular information. How this group has access to this office is a very serious matter and who knew that you were on the case. I only called you yesterday evening and for you arrive the day that it was reported is beyond a joke and how do they know the content of the investigation. Who knew that an MP was murdered? The local police on the case have not let events be known yet. It is still under wraps." "The only real lead that we have is that this department is the common source of the paperwork and of my involvement. Someone here has the start in answering some of the questions." "I don't see how anyone could have any knowledge because I did not tell anyone that you were to be involved. Wait, the paper advertisement but they don't know the code, or do they?" "I don't think that anyone could have known Sir but we could give out some false information and track any access to it. At least we might get a break through. If you send another code message?" "We could certainly try it. What do we send?" "If you send me another message in the same manner that you did the first time, we could track any access." "Right, we will do it now." Sir George went through the same procedure and they waited, tracking on all channels activated.

CHAPTER 21

Gerry Maidstone arrived home after leaving Whitehall with some work papers that needed his immediate attention. It had been a long day and he looked forward to the meal that his house keeper always made for him when he was going to be late. Sheila was a lovely woman who had taken to looking after Gerry, she lived just a few doors away and worked for pleasure as a house keeper, not for the money.

He sat down to his late dinner and was enjoying the prepared meal whilst going through the lists of staff who required new quarters after the leaked information of staff details. It was a matter of redirecting offices and accommodations in their department. He was feeling quite tired and as he finished his meal he retired to the lounge and poured a glass of Italian Rosso wine. Fatigue was causing his eyes to close but he was determined to enjoy his glass before giving and going up to bed. 'I have worked hard today and looked forward to this' he thought.

Sheila was returning from late night shopping, as she passed Gerry's front window, she saw that his light was on. 'He has arrived home at last' she thought and she stopped and knocked on his front door. There was no answer and she thought that maybe he had fallen asleep after his meal and left the light on by mistake. She would just pop in and turn off the lights. As she entered the house, she quietly called out Gerrys' name but there was no answer. As she entered the lounge to turn off the light, she saw Gerry sprawled out on the floor, he was covered in blood and had obviously been repeatedly stabbed and obviously dead. She stifled a scream but recovered quickly and called 999.

Inspector Brown stared at the body, "This is a copy death of the MP, with same repeated, savage attack to make sure that he was dead. Forensics needs to cheque any similarity in the details of the two murders. Have they been contacted?" "Yes Sir, they are on the way" confirmed Sergent Dawson. "Make sure that the photographer gets shots from every angle he can. I want this murderer caught. If I am right, this is the same person responsible. I see that all his work papers are still as he left them, nothing has been taken that I can see. I can envisage no motive for these killings unless he or she just likes to kill but it looks like the work of a man to me. Later the forensic department confirmed that there were too many elements common to both murders for it to be a coincidence. Their conclusion was that it was the same person who had committed both attacks.

Inspector Brown ordered background checks on the two victims to see if there was any connection between them and he wanted a check any movements of both. 'An MP and a Whitehall employee, what was the common factor or was there none?' he thought. There was nothing more to do on this until the reports came back so he headed for home. The next morning Inspector Brown got up and took the morning paper from the letter basket, glancing at the headline on the front page, "Whitehall worker hacked to death." He was astounded and very angry, "How the hell did they get that information? How does anyone know? Who could have said anything? Was there a leak in his force?" He called the Chief Constable immediately and told him of the newspaper report. The Chief Constable spluttered and coughed and told Brown to be in his office without delay. The phone went dead.

Back in his office he called his team together and told them to wait until he got back from the chiefs' office, with that he left. The Chief Constable had had time to think about events and had calmed down and stopped blaming Brown for something outside of their control. "Thank you for coming Brown, have you any thoughts on this?" "Not at the moment sir. I have gathered my team who should have the reports that I asked for yesterday, until I have a chance to go through them, I am as much in the dark as anybody. I can confirm that it is the same killer, backed up by forensics." "Very good Brown, keep me informed."

Inspector Brown entered his office to a complete silence. They had seen the newspaper report as well and were at a total loss.

Following his meeting Inspector Brown contacted Sir George with his conclusions. "Thank you for letting me know, in the circumstances we will make our own enquiries but I will keep you informed if we have anything that may be of interest to you. Sir George put down the receiver and immediately called and updated Huntley with the findings. Sir George was trying to come to terms with what had happened when his P.A. knocked and entered the office. "There is the Chief of Foreign Affairs to see you Sir." "Okay let him in." The Chief of Foreign Affairs was Rodney Philbin, an assistant to Sir George many years ago. He was a very ambitious and unpleasant character.

"Good to see you again Sir George." Sir George was taken aback when he saw who it was now in charge of such an important department. "What can I do for you Philbin?" "I have heard about these murders of yours, I just wondered if we could give you some help with it? It may be that there is an alien country involved and that is my department." "This is an internal matter and there is no evidence to support your theory. If evidence comes to suggest a foreign country is involved, I will let you know through the usual channels. Good day, Philbin." He left with a sour smile, slamming the door as he went. Sir George wondered why he had had a visit from Philbin, it was none of his business and totally out of tune with security matters. He always was an interfering individual but a personal visit was against normal procedure, strange.

He turned back to the situation in hand, two murders, connected by forensic evidence but not by occupation or circle of friends. As he pondered Huntley entered the office. "I hope that I am not intruding but I wondered if I could have a word?" "Come in Huntley I am glad to see you. You saved me the trouble of calling you. Sit down and tell me what is on your mind." "I have been going over the information and it became a rather dangerous and evil possibility. Both men were connected by their having lists of this departments staff details. It occurred to me that there may be more deaths Sir. The MP was on his way to his office to contact you about something to do with the list he had. I spoke to his P.A. and it was in his diary for that day, marked extremely urgent." Sir George thought for a moment, "I was looking for a connection between the victims and you have hit on it, and, carry on Huntley." "The fact that the news was out so quickly and may even have been before the murders, opens up a serious line of enquiry. I did not want to see anyone in their organisation as it might compromise my situation. The time scale on both murders is questionable. How did they get it so quickly? Can I leave that to you Sir?" "Can't Peter do that?" "He could sir, let me have a think about. Any other thoughts Sir?" "No just get on with it and keep me informed." "Yes Sir."

Huntley left the office and headed for his office in the main building. He very rarely used it but he had to contact Peter straight away to see if they could get together later. After his call to Peter, he headed home. He still had the disguise kit from his last investigation and it occurred to him that it was the ideal chance to use it again but not as a tramp this time. With glasses and whiskers and a strange looking nose he set off to meet Peter and head for the news agency that had been giving out news as it happened. Peter did not recognise Huntley as he was approached, only when Huntley spoke is when he recognised him. "What's this all about?" "I want to keep my identity secret from these news sharks, the less they know, the better. I just want to watch the news office for a while to get a feel of their operation. There is a coffee bar across the road from them, let's have a leisurely coffee." They sat for a while watching the activity across the road but not a lot was happening. A car stopped outside the news office and someone went to the news office door and ran back to the car. The car had obscured the person and the car had cut out in front of another car so that the number plate was not in view. They stayed watching for a few minutes but there was no further activity. "Time to give them a visit." Huntley left the café and went to the news office with Peter in tow. At the reception desk they asked to see the editor, "What is it that you want to see him about?" The receptionist was a mousey, bespectacled, middled aged man with a definite attitude. Huntley started to explain their visit but the receptionist interrupted, "He is far too busy, you need to make an appointment. Who shall I say called?" It was obvious that it was not going to be any good proceeding with the visit so Huntley just turned and left. It was clear that this little man had instructions not to allow anyone into the office which is not like any other newspaper office in whole of London. "Let's have a look around the building. You go that way Peter and I'll go this way, see if you see anything of interest." "Like what?" "Anything that is not normal in a newspaper office." They set off and met the other side of the building. They arrived outside of the print room window and they both spotted the head line on the header board, 'Westminster officer shot dead." They were astounded and they looked at each other in horror. "Let's get back to Westminster immediately." They both ran the half mile back to the office and straight into Sir Georges office with the news of their discovery. "There has not been any report of a death in the service, you must be mistaken or misread the board." "Not a chance Sir, we both saw the same header, it was no mistake." There was a knock at the door and the P.A. came in, quite flustered. "There has just been a shooting Sir, Lance Pearson has just been killed. He was just found outside the main gate." Stunned silence filled the office, they all came to the same conclusion at the same time. Huntley spluttered, "They are creating the news, not reporting it. We could

have the murderers." the team was gathered for a raid on the newspaper building and within two hours the raid was made. This time the little receptionist was more co-operative, as he had no choice and the editor was only too keen to talk. Huntley had not had time to remove his disguise so he challenged the editor, "How are you getting information before the event has taken place?" "I don't understand, we get reports from a variety of independent reporters and we take it to print." "You have a headline today on a murder before it had even taken place. How can that be?" "What are you talking about?" "Your header today is about a shooting in Whitehall and you had the headline before the shooting took place" "You can't be serious we print reports not predictions." "Where did you get your information from for todays' headline, by the way you can cut that print?" "Too late the papers are on the street with this evenings' delivery." "Get in touch with Sir George and slap a 'D' notice on it Peter. Who gave you the information and remember you are in a lot of trouble already?" "I will have to check." The editor went to his in tray. "It was' Truline' reporter." "The name?" "He is independent he just drops off the information and we send a cheque to his account. I don't think that I have met him." "Has anyone met him?" "I can't say." "Right team, I want any or all information on 'Truline'. Go through everything they have here any objections just lock them up." "You can't do that." "Yes, we can and will if we have to. I expect total co-operation from everyone here, is that clear?" Huntley left the team to do their work and headed back to see Sir George. "Did you get the message from Peter Sir?" "Yes, everyman we have is on the job and Scotland Yard are helping. What caused the panic?" "No panic Sir, it looks as if someone is feeding information to the newspaper and is totally unknown to them other than the name 'Truline'. That is if the editor is to be believed." "I see. It could be any individual, group or organisation providing the details of a murder yet to be done." "My thinking exactly Sir. Has Inspector Brown been contacted?" "Yes, he is on the case. He was called by the woman who heard but did not see the incident and found the body. She is in a bit of a state, I understand. You should talk to Brown and then I want you and Peter to get to work on solving this. It seems that there is a vendetta against my department as the victims are our men. The MP knew too much to be allowed to reach us. Maybe if he had we could have prevented these deaths." "Peter is still here, I take it. I will get this mask off and get on to it straight away Sir." Sir George nodded and Huntley left the office.

Peter and Huntley set a trap with the aid of the editor to try and identify the reporter. The little man on reception was replaced by an officer from their team and cameras fitted to get every angle possible of anyone dropping information at the newspaper door. Inspector Brown had been told of their plans and he had stationed police officers in strategic points to try and capture anyone dropping paperwork at the newspaper door.

They waited and waited and teams changed shifts to make sure that there was no gap in observation. It was three days later that there was action. Huntley and Peter were having a coffee opposite when a black cab pulled up outside of the news office and a man jumped out and ran for the door. The police on duty were quick to respond and as the man got to the door with paper in hand, he was taken into custody. Hunley was quickly over to the scene and grabbed the paper, it read, 'Another Whitehall worker stabbed to death.' Peter called the information in to Sir George. All personnel were alerted to the news and all were on full alert. There were no reports of anyone missing or hurt. The man who delivered was taken to Scotland Yard and questioned but it soon became clear that he was given the task and paid to deliver the message. He had been paid well and as he was unemployed and on the 'dole' he accepted the job.

In Whitehall everyone was on edge, Sheila, the office manager was with her senior officer discussing the situation. Sheila needed to go the ladies' toilet and excused herself for a few minutes. After ten minutes the senior officer asked Tammy to see where she was and Tammy headed for the toilets. Sheila was on the floor in a pool of blood and very dead.

Chapter 22

Sir George was in the office when Philbin burst in followed by the P.A. "Sorry Sir he just forced his way in and I couldn't stop him." "What is the meaning of this Philbin? How many staff are going to be killed before you do something about it?" he shouted. "I am still senior to you and you are way out of order bursting into my office like this. Get out before I have you put in custody." "You can't just sweep this under the carpet Curswell, I will make a complaint about the lack of action from your department." "Get out now." Philbin stormed out of the office, muttering as he went. "Sorry Sir, there was nothing that I could do." "If that clown comes again, feel free to call security and have him locked up." "Yes Sir." Sir Geoge knew that everyone was on edge but that sort of behaviour was unacceptable, particularly by Philbin. 'What was he thinking of? A head of one department interfering in another senior department.'

A call for Sir George took him upstairs to the Senior administrator, "Thank you for coming George. I have had a complaint that you refused help from Philbin and you have had three deaths in your department, all murdered. The claim is that you have done very little to find the culprit, Is that correct?" "Certainly not Gerry. Inspector brown of the yard has been involved and I have internal enquiries underway at this moment. I have had trouble with Philbin before but he has never gone beyond internal etiquette before. He is very ambitious and he doesn't care who gets hurt when climbing over people to get to his goal. I am surprised that he is in charge of a department here." "I see but I have had a complaint and I am bound to follow it up. I have done that so just get on with what you are doing and I will have a word with Philbin. I do not like his attitude either." "Thank you, Gerry." Sir George left the office and made his way back to his office.

The newspaper had been left to continue operations in the hope that it would lead to finding out who it was responsible for these murders. A round the clock watch had been put in place but Sir George knew that the messages were delivered by minions who didn't even know who they were working for. He did not have any confidence in that direction of enquiry. He wondered if Huntley and Peter had any information.

Huntley and Peter had investigated every possible avenue of enquiry but to no avail. The people who delivered the news to the paper had no idea who was responsible for providing it. The trail was cold and time had passed since the last murder. "It looks as if we have hit a brick wall Peter." "I agree there are just no leads to follow, whoever is responsible has been very thorough in covering their tracks." "I don't think Sir George is going to be very happy with our efforts Peter. "No, my brother has never been very understanding if he didn't get results."

True to form, Sir George ranted and raved for a time but no other members of the team had come forward with anything either and things settled down for a while. Huntley and Peter had had good results in other investigations but no matter how they tried, no information came to light on the murders. The press was still holding back on reporting as they still had a D notice in place due to the delicate security aspect. The possible reasoning for the murders could be from a foreign source.

Sir George took his early morning papers to his office and as he walked to his door, he saw that there was a memo from the Prime Minister. "Drat! I could do without this just now." He cursed as he sat at his desk. He picked up the phone and called the PM's office and made an appointment to see the PM.

"Ah George, do come in." "You wanted to see me Prime Minister?" "Yes, I understand that an MP was murdered?" "That is correct sir, also two of my department in the same manner." "I have seen nothing in the media." "No sir we have put a D notice on it for the time being as there may be some sensitive information involved." "What have you done about it then?" "Enquiries have been negative and the culprit or culprits have covered their activities very thoroughly. It is obviously a well organised group in my opinion." "The police have also been involved I understand." "Yes, we have kept them up to date with our findings and they have reciprocated sir. This is an internal matter and should not be interpreted as a political situation. I will keep you informed of any progress and the media will get the facts when we have them." "The reason that I asked you here is that I have had a complaint about your department from a unknown source." "That should tell you everything sir. An anonymous complaint." "Well, I can't just ignore it, I must follow it up as it is

my duty to check." "If that is all sir. I will let you know first when there is any real progress." Sir George turned and left without waiting for any response. 'I can I imagine who that informant was but I cannot substantiate it.' he thought as he made his way back to his office. Huntley was waiting for him to give a report on his findings. He also knew about the call to the PM. "How did it go sir?" "It is enough to make a saint swear, bloody cheek of it, an anonymous tip off to the PM and he takes it seriously. Where do they find these political cases?" "It looks to me that someone is waging against you or this department sir. It can't be Philbin sir, he couldn't be that stupid. He is the obvious choice but it can't be." "The same thought occurred to me. I know that he is an ambitious nuisance but he isn't that silly. He did threaten to complain however." "There is no evidence that it is a foreign activity either sir, I have looked through all the foreign activity reports and there is no activity that could be connected. Criminal groups are not operating in that field at the moment so it is a bit of a puzzle and there are no particular motives." "We have to get to the bottom of this, it is not good for the department. It could be just coincidence of course but very unlikely and the list of people in this department found on the MP must have some connection, keep digging Huntley." "I think that you have just hit on it. sir, the first death must be just the lead that we forgot to follow up. That could be it sir, we start again from scratch." Huntley called Peter and asked him to get the file from records on the MP murder case. Huntley called Inspector Brown to update him with all the information he could provide and requested all police records on the MP murder. Inspector Brown was happy to send him all that they had. Peter called to let Huntley know that the record office had no file on the MP murder. "They must have, I sent it to them myself." "Not according to the records officer. He remembers filing it but there is no trace of it now." "Someone has obviously taken them but how? Who has that clearance to access records? Philbin?" "I think that he is the most likely person after his actions of late." agreed Peter. "Okay Peter, I will go and see Sir George and update him. You take the rest of the day off."

Sir George could only agree with Huntley after being told about the latest event. "What has this Philbin chap got against you sir?" "I don't really know but he may have found that my original assessment of him after his training was

not very complimentary. Other than that, he is just an ambitious and amoral sort of person and my original assessment stands." "I can't see him resorting to murder to discredit you."

"One never knows, but I tend to agree with you." "How do we proceed sir?" "Let me thing this over. It is getting late so we will take it up again in the morning." "Have we any back up with the file on the MP murder?" "Yes, I have my copy of the police report and our own records. I will get my assistant to give you a copy as you leave." "Right sir, I will see you in the morning." Huntley went to the assistants' office and took the copy home. Huntley poured himself a large whiskey and sat down to read the file. The list of names on the body had to be the reason for his death. A copy of the list of all the department members. 'Who else had such a list?' thought Huntley. Thoughts came back to records office and who had access. He had to check who had requested a copy recently. As it was pleasant outdoors he decided to walk.

As he headed to check access to records, he passed a shop window and glanced at the sloping entrance window, he saw reflected a person in black clothing pointing a hand gun in his direction. He dived for the floor as the shot rang out. The glass window shattered and covered him in broken glass. He rolled into the shop doorway and looked back in the direction of the gun shot but the assailant was not to be seen. He was very shocked and a bit bruised but still in one piece. Assistants from the shop came out to see what had happened and helped him to his feet. "Was that a gun shot or a back fire?" enquired one of the shop assistants. "It was a shot fired from back there." said Huntley pointing in the direction of the place where he saw the assailant. The staff immediately made their apologies and went into the shop leaving him standing in shock. He headed back to the office and made the enquiry by telephone. 'Who was the gun man? Did he look familiar? Could it have been Philbin?' His mind raced with questions. Sir George was very shocked when he got the report and revised his opinion about Philbin. 'He is the only one I know with an axe to grind.' As he considered all the recent events there was a knock on the door and a messenger was ushered into the office. "Yes, can I help you?" "I have a message from the PM. He would like to see you immediately Sir." "What now?" "Straight away Sir."

Sir George entered the PMs' office to find Philbin stood next to the PM. "Do come in Sir George. Take a seat." He pointed to the low chair facing the window. An old trick to make a person feel pressurised. Sir George was fully aware of the ploy. "Philbin has something of yours. It was found in one of his departmental vehicles." The file was thrown onto the desk. It was obviously the file that Peter could not find. "You seem to be having a lot of problems with your department, can you explain this?" "Before we go any further, I object to a junior member being present while such matters are discussed." "It is Philbin who has found another mess in under your leadership." "You will have him leave before we continue with this matter. You should know the protocol in such things." "Thank you Philbin, I suppose that you should go." "Yes Sir." Philbin left, sickly smile on his face as he went. "That was very embarrassing Sir and should not have happened." "It does not alter the facts. You have had deaths, problems and now loss of record documents, found in a car of another department. You seem to have lost control of things." "There seem to be many factors that have escaped you and you have not enquired about the facts in this case. Bringing a junior and his accusations into an enquiry before ascertaining the evidence. We have reason to believe that Philbin may be involved with these events and he is certainly suspect in events. You may be associated with criminal actions accepting Philbin's versions of things. That could be misconstrued by the opposition if it gets out." The Prime Minister coughed and spluttered before apologising. "I'm sorry, Philbin was very convincing with his stories, I had no reason to disbelieve him." "He has an axe to grind over an assessment that I had to give when he was training. He may and I stress he may be involved with criminal acts. We do not have any proof at this time but there are concerning connections. We have ongoing enquiries which you will be the first to hear about the outcomes."

Chapter 23

Sir George returned to his office, still fuming with the PM and his blunders. Maybe that will keep him off my back for a while and Philbin will not have his ear from now on. He was now, more convinced that Philbin was involved and he decided that he would get the facts about him. How had he got hold of the file? He would find out. He picked up the phone, "Hello Huntley, come to my office as soon as possible." "I am on my way Sir." "Before you come here, bring Philbin with you." "It will be my pleasure Sir."

Philbin entered the office with the same sick smile. "You have made accusations and attempted to discredit my department. You have over stepped the mark this time." "The PM" Sir George cut him off before he could say anything else. "The PM nothing, you may leave this office as a clerk in your own department and handed over to police for investigation." Philbin blanched. "Whatever your reason for attacking my department, you had better forget them. How did you get the file and don't tell me that they were found by accident?" "But they were found in one of our cars on the front seat. I have no idea how they came to be there." "You took full advantage to discredit us. Which is not acceptable in any Whitehall circles. Your actions could link you to murders and attempted murder" "But that is ridiculous, I have had nothing to do with anything like that." "You may say that but it could be viewed that you have. You fail to see the seriousness of the situation. There are many possibilities for the attacks on my department, with the murders etcetera and your attempts at discrediting my department link you to them." "No, I may have had a grievance but I would never" "Then you had better start acting like a head of department and give support to our enquiries, which still does not clear you of anything. You will need to prove it." "I am sorry. I let my feelings get the better of me. I know that your assessment was correct but it hurt to be told the truth." "Now is the time to change all that. We need, as department heads, to work together. I don't have any reason to doubt what you say but you will have to show a definite change of attitude." "Yes Sir, sorry. I will give you a report on all our findings." Philbin left the office.

Huntley looked at Sir George. "Well Sir, I think that you spelled it out very clearly. I think that it was a case of kill or cure." Sir George was almost steaming and took a while to gather himself. "We need to go back to the newspaper to

see if we can get any leads there and continue your check on Philbin. I don't think that he has any connection to the murders but we can't rule him out yet, he may have hired someone." "Yes Sir, I will also get onto inspector Brown and see if he has anything further to help us."

Huntley met up with Peter and brought him up to date. "I can't believe all this. It is like something out of a novel. You just can't take it in." "I agree Peter, look, we will go and have something to eat and then get on with it. They talked and talked over the meal and Peter offered to take on some of their enquiries to lessen the load on Huntley. "Great Peter, I will go and see Brown first and then we will go the newspaper together." They left the newspaper office without gaining any further help. The staff were not very co-operative but as they left a van driver came over, "Hello, I heard that you were asking about people who delivered news items here." "That is correct, can you help us?" "There was a young man who made a couple of deliveries and he stood out from the others.

He was well dressed, dark to black hair and was not the type to be a delivery boy. Middle twenties and pin stripe suit, clean shaven." "Thank you. Any distinguishing marks or scars?" "A funny left eyebrow, as if a bit shaved off." "Thank you have been a great help." Back in the office Sir George was updated. "I have some news for you as well. Philbin had a girlfriend in Ragusa in Sicily and spent some time there. Francesca was associated with the Mafia there. It may be nothing but I think it needs checking. We have no one out there so you and Peter will have to go and find out what you can." "Are there any records of his time there?" "No, it was before he joined the service but he could still have connections." Huntley made return bookings to Comiso military airport through the R.A.F. The airport was about nine miles from Ragusa. He also arranged transport to Ragusa. Francesca Millotti lived on Via Risorgimento just past the creperie in Ragusa. They packed and set off for R.A.F. Northolt and arrived in Comiso late evening and spent the night there. The next morning, they set off with an allocated driver to meet Francesca. I would like to interview Francesca alone, two of us might be more than needed. I will meet you here in the creperie. Huntley left Peter at the creperie and headed for Francesca's house. As he passed Via Angelo Musco, he was aware of a glint of sun flash from the end of the road, instinct made him draw the gun he acquired before arriving. As he turned and stepped sideways, he saw the gunman at the corner. He dropped down and fired just as the gunman fired. He felt the rip of his shirt as the bullet passed through the sleeve. There was a shout of surprise from the gunman and he disappeared. Huntley waited to see if he appeared again and he heard a second shot and then seconds later, he heard Peter coming from the direction of the creperie and he saw him clutching his right arm. "I heard the shot and came to see if you okay but I nearly bumped into the gunman. I dropped down but not quick enough, I've been hit. He ran up Via Guastella and jumped into a waiting car." "Did you get a look at him?" "Yes, he fitted the description given by the van driver. He was dark, well dressed and his right eyebrow was missing a bit in the middle. I would definitely remember him if we meet again. I got a good look at him." "Come on let's get that wound seen to, I can call on Francesca later."

The military medics said that they would keep Peter in hospital for a couple of days to ensure that there were no complications. Hutley set off to see Francesca early the next morning. She was not at home but the next-door neighbour said that she was at her father's house. He owned a large villa on Via Giordano. Huntley headed up the hill to the villa to find Francesca with her father and brothers taking morning coffee. He explained his visit and he was welcomed to join them on the terrace. The coffee and Cantuccini were just right for a morning break. "I am sorry to trouble you but I am making enquiries on a MR. Philbin and your experience of his time here." Francesca's father Ricardo smiled and paused for some time. "He was in a relationship with Francesca but none of the family were happy about it and we were proved right." Francesca nodded. "He was ambitious and self-seeking, not to mention stupid." "That sounds like the chap that I am trying to get information about. It sounds as if he was not very appreciative of your daughter." "As you English say, he was a bounder and hot headed." "Was there anything in particular that stood out in his behavioural habits?" "He was most inconsiderate towards others and considered that he was superior to everyone else, he had to have his way or he became morose. He would retaliate in his own way to get back at anyone who thwarted him. He was stupid with my sons here and he was very lucky to leave here alive." "Thank you very much, I think that I have all the information I need but was he ever aggressive towards anyone?" "He did not have the courage to challenge anybody in the family, he was sly and not to be trusted." "Thank you, Ricardo, it was a pleasure to meet you and your family." "You must stay for lunch and we will show you around this afternoon."

"You are most generous it would be a pleasure." "How long will you be in Ragusa?" "At least two days. My friend was shot and wounded yesterday afternoon near Francesca's house. He is in the military hospital for a couple of days." Ricardo sat upright, "Did you get a look at the shooter?" "Yes, my friend saw him quite clearly. Young, well dressed and a missing part of hir right eyebrow." Ricardo looked at his sons and Francesca without any recognition from them. "I have not heard of anyone like that near Ragusa but if he is a new member of a group in Ragusa we will find out. You must spend your time with us while you are here and we will find your shooter man. I insist." Huntley was not going to argue or refuse such generosity from Ricardo. Huntley knew that Ricardo led a family group and had much influence in Ragusa and Sicily in general. "I am honoured." "You are most welcome. Bella, prepare a room for Mr. Huntley. I will arrange clothing for you and whatever else you need." The boys smiled and took turns to shake Huntley's hand. In his room Huntley considered events and realised that the family were pleased that he was possibly going to bring Philby to account. He smiled and realised that he was part of the team here for a while.

Chapter 24

Huntley was shown to his room. The room was spacious and led onto a wide balcony that overlooked south Ragusa and although they were some distance from the sea, the water sparkled in the distance. There was an En suite and a dressing room. There were all sorts of clothing, suits, casual, shirts, shoes and everything that was needed for every occasion. Huntley had never seen such luxury in his life, 'What a way to live' he thought. There was a knock at his door and Bella entered. "Mr Ricardo would like you to join him on the terrace, you have a visitor." "Thank you, do you know my visitor?" "No sir." Hunley quickly changed into casual clothing and went down to the terrace.

"Ah, Mr. Huntley, you have a visitor. Let me introduce to you Commissario Montello, he is interested in a shooting that you may know something about." "Good to meet you Commissario, how can I help you?" "Weare led to believe that you were involved in a shooting, how did you have a gun?" "I was shot at Commissario and my shirt has the evidence to prove it." Ricardo smiled and gave a feint nod. "So, our information that there was a shootout is incorrect?" "It would appear so Commissario. The assailant was a smartly dressed young man with dark hair and a part shaved right eyebrow and this was not his first attempt to kill me." "You English come to Italy and gave us many headaches." "Not as bad as the headache that I would have if he had succeeded." Ricardo interrupted, "Commissario Montello, you insult my guest in my house. He has had a bad experience in Ragusa you should be apologising for his discomfort in our home town." Montello coughed and realised his error. "I am sorry Mr. Ricardo, I was not thinking. I am sorry Mr. Huntley. We will do all that we can to find this dangerous person but you must know that we have many similar incidents." "My friend is in the military hospital after being shot by this man and he got a good look at him. You may be better speaking to Peter Curswell." "Thank you, Mr. Huntley. Thank you, Mr. Ricardo." The Commissario left looking quite sheepish, hoping that Ricardo would not make his life difficult. Ricardo smiled and shook Huntley by the hand, "You should be working for me, you dealt with that very well, things could have turned out very different." "Thank you, Ricardo." "Well now, let us take some lunch and we will show you around. Pietro, find this gun happy man of Huntley's." "Yes father." Pietro left and Ricardo explained that Pietro was very efficient in doing the right thing. Huntley wondered what was the right thing in this case. Huntley knew that Ricardo would not like anyone operating in his district without his approval. They finished lunch and spent the afternoon visiting interesting places and meeting some very interesting people. The evening was spent eating and drinking a lot of Montepulciano d'Abruzzo. Huntley wondered what his head would be like in the morning. He slept very well and woke with thunder in his brain but after a hearty breakfast it faded fast. Pietro, at breakfast had reported back that there had been no trace of the gunman. It was unusual that no one had seen or heard anything about him. Ricardo thought that this man must have very important connections to disappear without trace. There was no record of a person of his description arriving or leaving Sicily by air or sea. "This is not good news, no one gets to this place without me knowing." Ricardo was very angry and let Pietro know it. "Get back out there and find the man I will have him." Ricardo called the 'Fathers' together for an emergency meeting and they all arrived within the hour. The situation was explained and all attendees were equally angry that someone was operating without their knowledge. The meeting broke up quickly and they all set off in haste. Suddenly there was a serious situation in Raguso, every known villain in Ragusa had a visit from the powerful 'Fathers' in Sicily. The police were ordered to stay out of it and they complied without question, Commissario Montello must have been shaking in his shoes when he was told. Every avenue of search was followed but by the evening there was no news from any of the groups. Ricardo was seething and everyone was avoiding him. Huntley wondered if he was being held responsible for events but late evening the family and Huntley were called to the terrace for a drink. "Thank you everyone for your efforts. We will eventually find this man but as no one has any news. We must be up against a well organised group to be able to go under our system without detection. Thank you, Huntley for bringing our shortcomings to our attention. I wish you every success in your endeavours as I know that you will be leaving tomorrow with your friend Peter. The military will discharge him from hospital in the morning and your driver will pick you up at 0930 hrs. It has been a pleasure to spend time with you and I know that you will do the right thing with Philbin." They all raised their glasses to Huntley. Huntley was taken aback and just nodded and smiled. "If you ever come back to Ragusa, please come to stay with us." Ricardo shook hands.

The next morning all goodbyes were said and manly hugs all round when the car arrived for Huntley. Peter was in the car with his arm in a sling, "There is always a good side to things. I won't be able to do any reports for some time but I did give the police a good description of the gunman while I was in hospital." "They were not police they were Ricardo's men and they are in a right old flap." They arrived at the military airfield and boarded for home.

Back in Sir Georges office Huntley gave a briefing of events. Peter was sent to rest and recover. "That is the second time that you have been attacked. What I wonder is how this gunman knew you were in Sicily and how did he gain entry without someone identifying him? It is as if he is a ghost." "I left Ricardo and his men in quite a state they don't like anyone else operating in their territory. The report on Philbin is not good, did you get his report?" "Nothing yet but I hope that he sends it soon, he is on very thin ice as I have had reports of other petty happenings with other departments. Now you have confirmed that he has no connections with outside groups, it would seem that he is just unfit to be in Westminster and in a position as Head of Department. It is beyond me that after my report he had any sort of promotion. I do tend to disregard his involvement in the killings." "I do agree Sir, we are dealing with a very slippery character and I cannot see any motive other than to make you and this department look bad. Can you think of any past confrontations?" "There must be hundreds but none to warrant this sort of activity." "Looks like we are back to square one, again Sir." There was a knock at the door and the secretary came in and announced Inspector Brown. "Come in inspector, take a seat." Brown sat at the desk, "I thought that I would come to see you in person rather than send a message. We have made enquiries about the MP who was killed. He was looking for a file on security but the officer in charge was out of the office. Gerald Stone MP looked for the file himself and in doing so came across a list of your staff. Attached was another list with named members of your staff, numbered. He thought that it was strange so he was on his way to see you when he was killed. The numbered list was never found on him but we found it in his house in a locked draw. This is it Sir." He placed the list on Sir George's desk. Sir George scanned it and took a sharp intake of breath. "This numbered list is the order of staff murdered and there are more names numbered. You don't seem to be mentioned Huntley. Thank you, inspector, this is a very important step forward, you have done well." "My pleasure Sir." Brown got up and left the office.

"We now know why the MP, was killed, he had uncovered the plot before it had chance to get underway. Which office was it?" I am not sure, Huntley but I can easily find out." When you do Sir, we need to check who was working there at that time." "It's getting late Huntley and it has been a long day, I'll see you in the morning and I may have the information we need." "Very good Sir, goodnight."

The next morning came the news that Peter had an infection and had become very ill. The doctors were not sure what the problem was, so Peter had been taken into special care. The news was upsetting for Sir George and Huntley was very concerned for Peter. They had worked well together and Huntley was sorry that Peter had been injured whilst in his care. They talked about Peter and his rise to the department, "I tried to get Peter to work with me but he was not very keen, he thought that we might clash working together." "I can understand that Sir. Where did he work before he came to us?"" He was in the political civil service helping in a variety of areas and he was very well thought of by his superiors." "I am quite happy to work alone until Peter is fit for work again. I don't want him to think that we are replacing him while he is indisposed." "I agree Huntley but we need to make some progress with this case. The office where the MP came across the list was the filing office of the senior civil servant's department. Any one there had access to the files and the office itself, which is not much help to us but it is an avenue to follow." "Who gave the police all the information about the MP finding the list?" "Apparently the clerk to the registrar watches all visitors, very discretely, to ensure that when the office is empty, nothing untoward is going on." "Good on him Sir. I will go and have word with him and see if I can get anything else to help" Huntley set off to meet up with the clerk. His name was Edward Reeve and he was along serving member of staff in fact he was close to retirement. There was not much more that Edward could add to his police statement but he did say that Gerald Stone MP was a frequent visitor and was always checking events, in fact he always seemed to be ''on the ball'. The paperwork that the MP took was not departmental, it had been left by a previous visitor but he did not see who that was. Huntley set off for lunch and chose to eat where, nearly all, staff ate. As he sat down with his meal an old training buddy came over. "Hi, Huntley. How are you doing? I thought that you were with Sir Curswells' mob?" Ray Hackney, how are you? I haven't seen since training, what are you doing here?" "You first, where are you working?" "You are right, I am with Sir George and loving it. Now you." "I got a consultancy contract as a freelance advisor." "An advisor? You know nothing about anything." "Same old Hunley, even so that's what I do." "Great to hear it. You haven't changed a bit except that you have lost a lot of hair." "Thanks, I know that I could rely on you to bolster my confidence." "No offence intended." They laughed together and shook hands. "So, what are you doing with the 'Plebs'?" "I am following up a lead on the murders in our department and I have just had a chat with Mr. Reeve." "He is a right one Reeves, nothing gets past him. He knows more about the goings on here better that anybody else. Was he much help?" "Yes and no but he did give me a hope of finding something." "I remember those killings and that of Gerald Stone, I thought that your departmental deaths and Stones' death might be connected." "You may be right there. Do you move about in this place?" "Yes, do you mean do I know people working here? Yes, I do. Have you any particular names that you are after?" "I am after a face really. Young, well dressed and I mean well dressed in expensive stuff, very dark hair and a distinguishing, part missing eye brow over his right eye." "You have hit on two strange customers there. Two lads working here match that description, both spurious characters. I can't remember their names but I can soon find out for you. Give me your contact details and I will get them for you." "That's great, thank you." "Look I'm on my way to a meeting so I will let you get on with your lunch, I will be in touch." "See you later Ray." Ray headed off with Huntleys' email and telephone details. Later that day Huntley receive a message from Ray with the names and work details.

Sir George had a regular meeting at his club with other heads of departments. It was a great opportunity for interdepartmental information gathering. He set off for the car park, taking with him his briefcase and notes. As he approached his car, he realised that his wallet was still on his desk so he headed back to his office. Just before he reached the car park exit, there was a tremendous explosion behind him. He turned to see bits of his car crashing to the ground and the remains of his vehicle a raging inferno. He stood motionless, shocked to his core, had he got to his car as planned he would be in that blaze. It was now clear that someone had a grudge against him and wished him serious harm. 'Was that the bottom line in all of the recent events?' he mused, 'Was that the attempt to discredit his department with the killings?' Huntley had just arrived in his car at the car park entrance in time to witness the explosion and see Sir George motionless half way across the car park. He raced to help Sir George and as he called him, there was no response, he still remained totally shocked. Huntley shook him and Sir George gradually realised that he wasn't alone. "Are you okay Sir?" Sir George slowly nodded. "I saw what happened, was that your car?" He nodded again. Huntley walked him slowly to the office and on arrival poured him a large whisky which Sir George consumed with gusto. The medics arrived at Huntley's request and found that it was shock but no other physical injuries. As the medics left Sir George seemed to recover and explained his thoughts to Huntley. "I fully agree with you Sir, similar to my way of thinking, someone really has it in for you and is not bothered who suffers in the process." "Philbin has not sent that information he promised. I have my doubts about him as he has tried to discredit me before, maybe he has gone further than we thought in trying to harm me. All this for an honest report on his standards?" "I will go and give him a visit, even as head of department, he has to answer to my enquiries." Sir George nodded weakly and Huntley left the office.

Huntley arrived at Philbin's office but the P.A. could not help him, Philbin had not been in the office since he visited Sir George. There was no information as to his whereabouts even though the whole department had been making enquiries. Huntley left and headed for his office but then decided to go for a coffee in the 'Heaven and Hell' coffee bar in Old Compton Street. He strolled down Shaftsbury Avenue feeling quite puzzled about recent events. Peter in a recovery home, Philbin gone missing and Sir George barely avoiding being blown to pieces. He sat for, what seemed, ages sipping his coffee very slowly. None of it seemed to have any sensible explanation other than Philbin has been responsible for the attacks on his boss and employees but it now seems that he disappeared before the bomb attack.

He headed back to his office and was told by the receptionist that the Police were interviewing Sir George. Huntley quickly made his way to Sir George's office. Inspector Brown was there with two large constables, on the table was a large metal case looking as if it had been in the wars. Sir Gorge was looking at the case in bewilderment, "I have never seen it before." "Can you deny that the

initials are yours?" "No but GC could be anybody." "It was found in the boot of your car so how can it not be yours?" "I have no idea." The inspector opened the unlocked box, it was heavily lined with insulation and in the centre there were two large packets of white powder. "And I suppose you know nothing about the contents and their street value?" Sir George looked shocked and could not comment. The shock of the explosion and the shock of the Police interview was taking a toll on him. "I have no option but to arrest you for dealing in drugs, Constable." Sir George was led from the room under arrest. The police demanded the keys to Sir George's house to search for any other evidence involving drugs. Sir George told them that he only went to the house to pick up any mail. He had not lived there since his wife had died a few years ago. Even Huntley had not known that about Sir George and it came as quite a surprise but it explained why he was always using his office accommodation. Inspector Brown said that he was amazed that the evidence was so conclusive against Sir George, "I cannot believe that he would be involved with anything like this but the evidence is so damning, I have no choice but to arrest him." Huntley replied, "I am sure that he is totally innocent of anything illegal. He has had an attempt on his life and he has been through unfounded accusations in order to discredit him. He has been set up and I will prove it." "I hope that you are correct Huntley and from the start, things have not added up right." The inspector left Huntley shocked and angry but spinning with possibilities. He did not have Peter to help him so it would be up to him to get any results.

A day later and no further ahead, Huntley set of to the police station to see Sir George but when he made enquiries, inspector

Brown came to see him. "I had to be the first to tell you and it grieves me to have to do so but we searched Sir George's house and we found no evidence of drugs but we did find two bodies buried in his garden." "What? That just can't be." "It looks like Philbin and a small-time drugs dealer. We have his sister in for interview now. Would you like to be there when we question her?" "Sure thing, thank you inspector." "The bodies had been buried a couple of days by the look of things, they were not in good condition." They went to the interview room. A young well dressed, woman was in tears at the table. "Did you identify your brother?" The girl nodded. "When did you last see him?" It took some time for her to answer, "Three days ago. He always came for a meal at my place because he lived out of the frying pan all of the time and I told him it was bad for him." She broke down in tears again. The inspector gave her time to settle again. "Did he say anything about what he was doing?" "Yes, he was quite excited. He said that he had done some work for someone called Curston." "Not Curswell? "Yes, that's it, Curswell. He did some deliveries to a newspaper for him and he was excited that he had hit the big time with a drugs deal but I haven't seen him since." The inspector looked at Huntley, they were both quite stunned by this information. It was even more condemnation. "Constable, get this young lady a cup of tea and see that she gets home safely." They both left the interview room and went to Brown's office. "Things look very black for your boss Huntley. The evidence now points to Sir George setting up the paper murders and it looks as if he killed the drug dealer and the other one who turns out to be Philbin. They were both buried at the bottom of his garden." "I just cannot believe any of this. I don't know how but it has been so cleverly done to point the finger at Sir George all the evidence now coming together to condemn him." "I hear what you are saying but there is no other explanation." "There has to be and I will find it and prove his innocence." "I wish you all the luck in the world but?"

Huntley pondered for hours but nothing could explain anything away. All his possibilities seemed to crash as soon as he considered them. Hours passed and then a though hit him like a ton of bricks. He had to go back to Sicily to make further enquiries. He packed and took the first available flight. To his surprise as he checked through customs, a friendly voice called to him. "I see that you can't stay away Huntley." Huntley turned to see Ricardo give him a friendly wave. "Hello, my friend. How did you know I was coming?" "As you know, nobody arrives here without me knowing." "I think you are right and I may have some information to prove that." They drove back to Ricardo's house and Huntley was greeted by the family including Francesca. They had an evening meal and drank a number of bottles of Montepulciano d'abruzzo wine. "I am sorry I cannot tell you my theory at the moment, I need to check things first. I can tell you that Philbin is dead." Sounds of satisfaction sounded around the room but there was no comment. "Did you look for a gun at the creperie?" "No, we had no cause to." "First thing tomorrow can we go and look?" Ricardo called his eldest son over and whispered something to him. The boy disappeared quickly and the drinking continued. Within the hour the boy returned with a package. "Is that what I think it is Ricardo?" "It certainly is." "Can you have it fingerprinted?" "Of course, we can, we are not backward here." "I did not doubt you. I would not have asked if I thought that you couldn't." "We will have the results in the morning. Now let us rest for the night, your room is the same as last time and all ready for you." "Many thanks, Ricardo." The next morning Huntley was accompanied to see the doctor who had treated Peter and Huntley made some notes. "Thank you, Ricardo I have the information that

I needed. Now, I must get back home urgently. I will give you my findings as soon as I have them confirmed. I can tell you with some confidence that your people did not miss the well-dressed young man." "I will send the prints to you immediately I get them." They shook hands and Huntley left for the airport. The flight home was a long flight in Huntley's mind but he was eager to put everything together as quickly as possible for Sir George's sake. He was now beginning to understand what had happened but he could not attach any motive to his theory. When he got back to his office, a fax was waiting for him. It was the result of the finger print check. Huntley passed them on to his departmental staff for a specific check. Things were starting to come together at last but he had to speak to Sir George when the checks were complete. The situation was becoming very delicate and though there was evidence, as yet there was no proof.

CHAPTER 25

Huntley arrived back and headed for the Police headquarters. He arranged with Inspector Brown to be able to visit Sir George in the following week. He left the Police station and went back Sir George's office. He asked the secretary for the file on Peter Curswell and sat in Sir George's office to study it. None of the files could be taken out of this office. He read through all the information but it struck him that there was nothing prior to Peter joining Records in !962. There was a note scribbled in the margin saying that Sir George had received a recent memo telling him of a Peter Edward Curswell working in the Records Office. The date was very close to Peter joining Huntley. It looked as if Sir George had only just discovered his brother at that time.

The secretary knocked and entered the office, "There is a message for you." He placed an envelope on the desk and left. Huntley opened it and read the contents, it was from Ricardo, it read, 'It would seem that you were right. The finger prints were as you suspected. Good luck. Ricardo.' Huntley read it with some remorse and folded the message and put it in his pocket. He left, thanking the secretary for his help. Back in his office he called in two of his best agents and gave them the task of searching for information on Peter's background before 1962. He called Peter's previous head of department and made enquiries about time spent in records. The head of department said that a full report would be sent before the end of the day. Huntley had to have time to think and he headed to the embankment. He walked for ages and eventually went for a coffee and sat pondering over it and only came to drink it when it was cold. He hadn't realised that he had been sat there for so long. It was becoming very clear that the 'status quo. was no longer. With the information starting to come together, it was taking a turn for the worst scenario. Dare he conclude that Peter was at the centre of events and he was involved in something that was far reaching and dangerous. What could he say to Sir George? He had only recently discovered his brother, how far was Peter involved? Huntley needed more information there were too many gaps to provide the full picture. Against his better judgement, he had to speak to Sir George as soon as possible. He headed back to the Police Headquarters. Huntley asked Brown to be present while Huntley spoke to Sir George. "Tell me about Peter Sir." "How is Peter?" "He is recovering well and should be back at work in a few days. The doctors said that the wound to his upper arm became infected which caused him to be so ill but he is on the mend." "That's good. What do you want to know about Peter?" "Tell me what you know of him." "Well, I was born before the second world war in Peterborough but my father got a well-paid job in British steel and we moved to Parliament Road in Middlesbrough. The war started in 1939 and my father was called up to army and was sent down South. He came home sometimes but not often. The last time I saw him was in 1941. Mother became pregnant with Peter and he was born in 1942 in the Parkside hospital in Middlesbrough." "What a small world, I was born in Park Lane the same year at home only a few yards from the hospital. Carry-on Sir." Sir George continued. "I was sent to aunt Esme as my mother could not cope with me as well as the baby and just after Peter was born, the news came that my father had been killed in action. My mother was devastated and she seemed to give up and died soon after. Peter was adopted by a couple in Linthorpe, Middlesbrough and I did not see him after that. The next that I knew of Peter was a memo from records stating that Peter was working in that department. I was so happy that I had him transferred to help you." "Thank you, Sir, we will be back to see you soon and you will be out of here." They both left. "Why did you say he would be freed soon?" "Because he is totally innocent of any charges. I have a few enquiries to do and if you would like to be with me, I would be very pleased." "It is my investigation after all so I don't see why not."

They travelled to Middlesbrough the next day and headed for the registrar's office. After telling the registrar of their enquiry he gave them access to all records. They found the birth certificate of Peter but they also found the death certificate. Huntley stared in disbelief and so did Inspector Brown. Peter had caught T.B. aged three and died soon after. "Now it starts to make sense." said Huntley. "All of this is a plot against Sir George but who is Peter really?" "I will make a call to my station to have Peter or whoever he is, arrested." "Yes, we need to question him immediately." They caught the next train back to London and at the office, they were told that Peter had gone from his room and had not been seen for two days. "How did he know that we were onto him?" The inspector shook his head. "He can't be working alone. He has to have help doing what he did. It makes sense now how the newspaper got the news before it happened. It explains why the M.P. had to die and also the people in

our department. They all had information regarding Peter. I will explain in time. We have to find this imposter." "I will put out an all points alert. We have to find him as soon as possible. We also need to release Sir George, at least on bail if nothing else. He has been well and truly set up by this man. Do not forget that if Sir George had not delayed getting to his car, he would have gone up with it." "I agree, I can release him for further investigation. You were right he will be free the next time we see him." Sir George was so relieved to be out of his prison cell. "I owe you one." he said to Huntley. "I did not believe you after you left but you kept your word, thank you. How did you do it?" "I have some bad news for you, Sir, Peter died in his early years, in fact, 1945. The man you thought was Peter is an imposter and very dangerous one at that. He was responsible for all the deaths and no doubt, the drugs as well. The dealer's sister confirmed that the 'Big Hit' as she called it was with a man called Curswell." "I see, she would not know that there were two of us. It was difficult to believe I would be back in my office now." There was a knock on the door and the secretary came in with a message from inspector Brown. Huntley read it. "Great news, the imposter has been seen and is in a flat in Finsbury Park on Rock Street. We will head there straight away. The police have the place surrounded." "I am coming with you." They both set off and arrived very quickly to see armed police all over the road, surrounding buildings and accesses. Inspector Brown gave the order to move in and the man was taken totally by surprise and frog marched out of the building. He was hand cuffed and put in the rear seat of Sir George's car. "Why?" said sir George. "What did I do to you?" "You bastard, you killed the one man I ever loved. Godfrey, Godfrey Bellinger was my best friend and lover and you shot him." Huntley stepped in. "Who were you working with?" "They will still get you no matter what happens to me, I left them directions." He put his head in his hands and cried. They could feel no pity for him and as they turned to continue, they saw him froth at the mouth and he died in seconds. "He must have had tablets on him. Why did they not search him when they arrested him?" "Too late now." "What we do know is that it goes back to the purge on foreign agents in Whitehall. Bellinger was part of the Russian network which means that some of them are still operative." "You are right, Huntley. It looks as if we are back to square one rooting out foreign agents in Whitehall." "That is not the only possibility, Sir. He told us of his sexual tendencies, so it may not have anything to do with the Russian group." "Mm, yes, you could be right but how do we continue?" "He must be known in some of the groups in London. A man like that has to have friends of the same tendencies. I will get Brown onto it straight away. He has access to all of the information on such groups."

Inspector Brown passed on the information to his area stations to try and establish the group that the false Peter had been associated with. The problem was that his real name was an unknown entity and if he didn't use the name Peter, then, things may be difficult. Photographs were circulated which may be the key to finding his group but there were so many unknowns. Brown was furious with his force for not finding the poison that Peter had used before being secured in the car and his team were very keen to redeem themselves. They set about their task with determination. It did not take them long after pulling out all the stops to find their target. The group frequented the 'Heaven and Hell' coffee bar in Soho and undercover police were frequent visitors and came up with the information as soon as they heard the instructions from H.Q. It took some time to identify all of the people involved but they were soon known by name and a file were raised on each member. The undercover officers knew many of the group and only two of them had any strength of character, the others were true followers and were not really capable of any original thought or action. The two names, along with the others, were passed on as possible contenders to H.Q. and inspector Brown joined Huntley to put together a plan of action. Kevin Trax and Mark Plant were known trouble makers and from the files, there was lists of police involvement. There was a repeating event shown on both files pertaining to the 'Union Club' just off pall Mall. "Inspector, I am sure that you know about the Union Club incidences?" "Yes, they were both accused of being in the club without invitation." "They must have been visiting someone as there seems to be many visits by invitation but there is no mention of who gave them the access. My officers have also noted that both of them were visitors to Westminster and again they were invited by some unknown person." "That must have been Peter. Did you get any information on Peters real name?" "Not yet but we should know something today." As expected, the news came that Peter's real name was Karl Dupart. Karl was known to have a record for fraud and deception and was a known, close friend, of Godfrey Bellinger. Huntley was not surprised at the news but was pleased to have a name for the imposter. Huntley set off to follow up on the two identified by the undercover team. The inspector headed for his office, he needed to catch up on all of the reports from his teams. Things were starting to make sense, at last, it all goes back to the Russian spy ring. Karl Dupart cannot be the master mind behind all of the past events, although, he could have headed up the group who murdered and set up Sir George. Where could he have been getting his instructions from? Karl's plans for continuing his attacks should have been nipped in the bud now that his group has been identified, all of them were now in custody. It became obvious that Karl had been used because of his association with Bellinger and was not really the main threat to Sir George, that was still active. At least whoever it is will now have to use a different plan, but what plan? The only clue left is the spy ring. Sir George may have been right when he said 'back to square one' but not quite. Huntley gave orders to his team to follow up on the two suspects and headed to Sir George's office in order to update him. They discussed all possibilities after Huntley had given his report and settled with the conclusion that there must still be Russian mole in Whitehall but where? All department heads had to be told and a meeting was set for the morning. It had been a tiring day and they left it all to tomorrow. On his way back home, Huntley strolled down the embankment and mused over the fact that a fraud Peter had been with him. He thought back to Sicily and the attempt on his life and it was now proven that it was Karl who shot at him and Huntley had inflicted the wound that put him in hospital. The finger prints on the gun found near the café were Karls. There was no smart suit after them, Karl had created him. Huntley smarted at falling for the deceit. Ricardo and his family had been right when they said that they could not find any evidence of any young man on the island. He would have to let Ricardo know. He slept as soon as his head hit the pillow.

The meeting started with heads of department looking at each other when told of a possible mole. Each firmly believed that it had to be another department, not theirs. Sir George asked each of them to not tell their people but to set up an enquiry into activities that may be questionable. They were not happy but agreed to produce a report before the next meeting set for the following week. It was stressed that it was a possible national emergency and personalities were not involved but the threat was real and the recent deaths were a result of this person's activities. Sir George informed them that they may be the next target. This information brought them together in their resolve to find the culprit. The meeting broke up and they all set off with a new determination. "Well done, Sir, they certainly got the message." "We need a joint effort with everyone on the same page." "I will go and see if Inspector Brown has any news." "Very good Huntley, I will be in my office." Inspector Brown had some of the reports back and was reading through them when Huntley arrived. "Hello Huntley, I have just gone through some reports and it has come to light that Trax and Plant were acting as rent boys to a number of members of the Union Club." "It could have been any number of members who signed them in to the Club, which doesn't help us very much." "True but there are many more reports to come in so it may be a lead after all." "You are right, Brown, I am not dismissing any possibility at the moment. What about the others in the group?" "It looks as if someone was getting them dates and making money out of their activities but no leads on whoever it was yet." "Have you any names of their clients?" "Some names have come up but none of significance as yet. As soon as we get more, I will get checks done on them all." "Great, good work Brown. Let me know if when you have anything." Inspector Brown set in motion a wide spread search throughout London and any outside connections to the case and waited for any response. Huntley set off for the office to report to Sir George and following his update, Huntley made a suggestion, "Sir, I need to see Ricardo again as he was a great help in uncovering Karl and his fraud. Would you like to have a break and visit him with me?" "I don't think that we can leave the case as it is." "We certainly could after your experiences and Inspector Brown is handling the situation very well. He will let us know if there is anything for our attention. I will leave him a contact number if he needs to contact us." "I think that you are right Huntley and I do need to get away from this for a while. We may come back to it refreshed. I will make the arrangements and we will leave in the morning. Do you need to get in touch with Ricardo before we set off?" "Ricardo will know the moment we step onto Sicilian soil."

CHAPTER 26

As they left customs at the airport, Huntley spotted a name card being waved. The card had Haverstock printed on it and it was being waved enthusiastically. "I told you that we need not let Ricardo know that we were arriving here, look." Sir George saw the card waving about, "How does he know?" "No one gets into the country without his knowledge. Come on there will be a car waiting to take us to his house." It was the eldest boy who drove them to Ricardo's and on arrival, he took their bags to rooms already allocated to them. "Thank you. We don't know your name." "I just get Boy, sir." "Thank you anyway." Ricardo greeted them enthusiastically, "This must be Sir George. Great to meet you and Huntley, how are you, my friend?" "All the better for seeing you." "Come, I am sure that you would like some real food after your flight. Would you like to freshen up first or would you like to eat?" "Give us ten minutes and we will join you on the terrace." "Great, I will make the necessary arrangements." "I have lots to tell you when we come down." Huntley knew the way to their rooms and Sir George was very impressed by his surroundings. "Ricardo must be very wealthy to have a place like this." "You do know what he does, don't you?" "You didn't say." "Ricardo is one of the top leaders in Sicily and he just about controls everything here, in all fields." "Ah, I understand, Mafia?" "I don't think that that word is ever uttered here but you are right."

At dinner Huntley told Ricardo of all that had happened and how Peter had died by his own hand. Ricardo was amazed at the related events and said "It seems worse than Sicily, deaths, intrigue and corruption. If it were in Sicily, the family would have sorted it much quicker." They all laughed and Ricardo raised a toast to Sicily. Huntley raised a toast to Sir George after all of his tribulations and incarceration. "To Sir George." Said Ricardo and the family gave a cheer. Sir George gave his thanks to the family and praised them for their welcome and hospitality. The drink flowed freely and tales of the family became more and more explicit but nobody really noticed. The morning was delayed because of flu symptoms or maybe alcohol abuse. Santa Grosse Camerina was the aim for the day. Ricardo had a Business there that needed his attention and Huntley and Sir George were invited to join him. They headed down to SP25 towards the sea and Santa Grosse Camerina. Not a lot was said but Huntley and Sir George were interested to see the Sicilian countryside. The road was good and the houses alongside were impressive. Large Villas and wide-open spaces made the blue sky seem like a vast canopy above them. After half an hour drive the group were feeling a little better from the fresh air drifting through their vehicles on the journey. As they entered the town there was the sound of a rifle shot, the front window next to Huntley showed a strike on the bullet proof glass. Ricardo called a halt and the other cars emptied as the occupants got out with guns raised. The group scoured the area but there was no sign of anybody. "We haven't had any trouble in this area for ears, what was that all about?" Ricardo looked at the strike on the front window, "It could have been a random shot but it could have been aimed for any one of us. Tell Peppo to get his men to find the culprit." Peppo was the local grandfather and had no issues with Ricardo as he did very well from the help that Ricardo had given him and continued to do so. There was no question that it was none of Peppo's men. "Did anyone see anything?" There was total silence. "I think we should leave it up to the locals to sort this and we will cancel our trip and head back. I am very sorry that this should happen to you in Sicily, I can only apologise." "No need, these things happen and we don't know what the motive was or who was the target." replied Huntley. When they returned there was a message from Peppo. It read, 'A man had been seen waiting next to a motor bike and was recognised by one of my men. The man was the one who came to Sicily with Haverstock.' Sir George gasped, "But that is impossible, we were there when Peter died." Huntley replied, "We need to get back to the U.K. without delay and check the findings of Peter's death. If he is here in Sicily, then something is not right in the U.K. I am sure that Ricardo will find this man if he is still here. Thank you for your hospitality and we are sorry to miss time with you but this changes everything. We need to leave immediately." Ricardo nodded and made arrangements for their journey. "If this man is still in Sicily, my men will find him." They thanked Ricardo and left for the airport.

CHAPTER 27

Back in the office Sir George contacted all of those in volved for reports on their progress. The Corroners' report was first and most important. The man who died in front of them was a twin and from dental records we found his name to be Alan Beard and his twin is Trevor Beard. The boys were born in Chelsea and worked together in an office as clerks in Government administration. As soon as the rest of the report was completed, it became clear that Peter was not Sir Georges brother after all but someone posing as a brother. Looking back with this information, things started to click into place. The attempt on Huntley's life had to be Trevor Beard. The confusion in their investigation had to be down to him as well and mis-direction became clear. Who was behind him? He could not possibly have been substituted as Sir Georges' brother without help. Someone else is involved and someone with plenty of influence. Peter is obviously still alive and hunting Sir George and Huntley. Huntley feared that this was a group and not a few individuals or someone who commanded a group. After all the reports were heard, Huntley and Sir George were alone. "How did you become aware that you had a brother, I thought that you said that you were an only one?" "There was a rumour that my mother had had another child but no one ever talked about it. Later, of course, we found that Peter had been adopted. I had a memo from admin. saying that there was a Peter Curswell working in their department. Later I had an unsigned memo that informed me that he was my long-lost brother. I had no reason not to accept it." "There is plenty of possibilities from what you say. Did records agree with the information?" "Oh yes. From the information on his C.V., his father and mother were also mine." "We now know that it was not true, he was Trevor Beard. Someone had to fabricate that information and even produce a false birth certificate but why? What is the motive for such a round-about method. It was originally to discredit you by setting you up with murder. I must have been just someone in the way." "We will have to find out who adopted Peter and what happened to him. I will get onto that immediately." Huntley left the office and headed for his. On arrival the secretary had a message for Huntley. "The man in Sicily was taken by Ricardo's men and when they got him in the car, he took a poison pill and died in the car." "Thank you," said Huntley, "That is the second death by their own hand. It looks as if, at last, this investigation is over." Huntley picked up the phone and contacted Sir Georgs to let him know what had happened. "Yes, Huntley, I got the same message. I do hope that we can put this to bed at last."

"Let's hope so sir." Huntley still had to establish what had happened to the real Peter and set off to records. He found that Peter had been adopted soon after birth by a couple who lived in London, Church Street in Windsor. The name of the couple was not listed but Huntley thought that he could research the house. He found that it was classified information and there was no record of the occupants. "Strange," thought Huntley," Why is it so covert?" The mystery was obviously not at an end. He travelled to Church Street and made enquiries. After hours of knocking on doors, many of which were Royal or State owned, he could find no record of a couple living anywhere in the Street. He went back to records and looked for any trace of a Peter Curswell, all he found caused him a sharp intake of breath. A Peter Curswell died, aged 6 months, of Pneumonia. Who could have known? How did the Beard twins take on the name? Why would they? It raised so many questions. He needed to think, so he headed for the restaurant on the embankment but realised that it was being redeveloped and had been knocked down. He headed for the Union Club, St. James Street. He dined there and took a room for the night. It gave him time to think as most occupants kept themselves to themselves, many of them leading industrialists or Government employees who did not want to get into any sort of conversation. It became clear to him that the Beards were only pawns in this affair and so were the others involved. The head of this organisation had an issue with Sir George and had somehow used these people to dishonour or even kill Sir George. Whoever it was had much influence and power. Huntley needed to go back over Sir Georges' career and see who had been affected by events. It would take some time as his career went back a long way and well before Huntley became Huntley. He left his room and went to reception and paid the account for his stay. He thought that he should check his bank account after his expensive stay. He knew he was well placed and had more than enough in his account but when he checked his balance, he was speechless. He had estimated a balance of hundreds but the balance was close to a million pounds. He could not believe what he saw. Where did that come from, not Ricardo or the office or any other place that he could think of. He went back to the office and on arrival people were astonished to see him. Everyone had been trying to contact him. There was an urgent summons from Sir George wanting to see Huntley without delay. The massage was twenty-four hours old and the office was in panic when no one could find him. He headed for Sir George. "Where the hell have you been? I sent the message yesterday." "Sorry Sir, I had to think and spent some time at the club." "Never mind think, have you checked your bank account?" "Yes, Sir and I was amazed." "You should be, there are thousands and thousands of unaccounted funds there." "I know Sir but I cannot explain it." "Neither can I. There are the same thousands in my account." "What?" They looked at each other in bewilderment. Huntley broke the silence and told of his findings. "There has to be a very powerful enemy from your past who has an axe to grind. This money has to be reported to the police before any accusations can be made." "I agree. I will get onto it now." Inspector Brown answered his phone and was surprised to hear Sir George tell of their fortunes and the unexplained monies in their bank accounts. "Can you find out how and who placed the money in our accounts?" "I am sure that we can get to the bottom of this Sir George." "I will leave it in your capable hands." Sir George put down the phone. "I must have upset somebody in my time." "I think that you are right Sir. I was thinking about that when I booked into the Club. I will get back to trying to find out who, in your past could possibly be responsible for it all." "I will go through my records as well but I can't think who has such a vendetta." Huntley left the office. He could not help feeling that he was being watched or followed as he walked down the Embankment. The person responsible had ordered that he should be killed before and that was on his mind that he might be a target again. He casually made his way looking for an opportunity to take evasive action and confirm that he was not alone. He turned into the Scotland Yard gate and quickly hid against the strut in the wall and waited. After five minutes, no one had appeared and he felt a little embarrassed at his actions but better safe than sorry. He continued his walk and considered his plan to find the culprit. After spending time walking and musing he found himself back at the House of Parliament and he went up the steps to Westminster Bridge and he glanced back to the Thames just in time to see a figure dart back out of sight. He wasn't imagining it, he was being followed. He dashed back down the steps but he could not see any suspicious figures anywhere in sight. He knew that he was not mistaken, he was being tracked by someone. 'Not another one of this gang after him', he thought. Ir still isn't over and we have not seen off all of the gang. Back in his office he enlisted the help of members of the department to trace back all of the cases in which Sir George had been involved. As it was getting dark now, he decided that he would go for a meal at Old Shades and then head back o his apartment. He had not been to Old Shades for such a long time and the place had changed but his favourite window table was still there and as he ate his meal, he saw the figure pass the window at speed. He did not get a good look but he was sure that it was a woman. The figure was hooded and wearing a Trech coat but there was no mistaking the gait of a woman. He knew that pursuit would be futile so he carried on eating but he would report to Sir George in the morning. The rest of the evening was uneventful and after a good night rest he called and reported yesterday's events. Back in his office there was a list of cases that might be of interest to a possible. He spent all day going through the files but nothing stood out as particular interest. There were more files to come and later that day they arrived in bulk. He needed some help with this and called Sir George for a recommendation. "The only person that would really be of help is someone who was with me in the old days, before you became Huntley and that has to be Tony Grey. I will get in touch and see if he is available." Huntley carried on through the mountain of files and after spending the whole day on his task he gave it a rest and headed for home. The next morning at the office Tony Grey was waiting for Huntley. Tony introduced himself and they ordered a coffee and sat down to exchange notes. "We need to make sure that we know who is who and not have the same identification, what do you suggest?" Huntley paused before answering, "As you are Tony, I will be Freddy and let Sir George know. Is that okay with you?" "Sounds good to me." F sent a memo to Sir George.

They got to work on the files. Tony had the old files and Freddy the files that he had had an involvement. As the day came to a close, they had a set of possibilities and headed for dinner to discuss them Not noticing the time the restaurant manager informed them that the staff were waiting to tidy up for the night, so they headed out. Tony was staying at Sir Georges guest apartment and so they parted and arranged to meet up the next day. The next day Freddy told Tony about his encounter with the mystery woman. "I went through some of the old files with Sir George and we couldn't find anything that remotely related to this case. The violence and scale of killing is beyond any previous experience. We discussed this case and the only one that related in any way, was the Bellinger affair." "Great minds think alike, I came to the same conclusion but there are few survivors from that affair and I could not come up with any party involved that would have such an axe to grind. I checked and there is no evidence of Russan involvement. It all seems to be all internal people taking part but the leader is a mystery. The girl that I mentioned may not even be a part of it." "Having talked to Sir George, it might help if you go through the Bellingham affair, I know very little of the events." "How long have you got? It was a very complex set of circumstances." "I have all day but I am due home in the morning." "I was a navigator in the R.A.F. and flew with Master Pilot Pinky James. He was a world-war two ace. We were on the supply support team for the BFPO forces in Germany. Every Tuesday we flew to Wildenrath, Weberg with supplies. It was so boring that we stayed over while the kite was checked for faults. We spent many an evening in the mess because going into town, there was still bad feeling from residents when they saw our uniforms. One night in the mess we were approached by two very smart girls and they were very obliging with their favours, if you know what I mean. It became a regular meet with the girls and something to look forward to. The mess barman was a pleasant young lad who introduced us to a cheap supply of boose and fags. We made a lot of money from that but what we didn't know was, we had been caught in a honey trap and we were blackmailed into doing things that we were not happy with." "That is when you tried to get out of going to Wildenrath again?" "Yes, we approached out C.O. and were imprisoned in a place near Marham Station and forced to fly a Constellation aircraft, Pinky had flown them before so we were trapped into flying the crate. We had to fly into Wildenrath again to pick up a whole lot of gear and also passengers. It turned out that we carried Castro into Cuba with a lot of Russian equipment. We were told to head into the U.S.A. after dropping them off but we didn't realise until we got into the air that we were along and sealed in. It was only that Pinky knew where there were spare parachutes were stored and an escape hatch location that saved our lives. We had just managed to get out and deploy the shuts before the Constellation exploded." "You were lucky to escape." "Yes, without Pinky's knowledge we would have been in the kite when it blew up. They must have thought that we were dead. They had already removed any records of our existence in the U.K. We were lucky also to find a whole fortune of bank bonds in their kit that they left in the Constellation and we were able to buy transport near Dallas to get around the States. Unfortunately, that was a mistake as they could track the banks that where we changed the bonds and realised that we had escaped. We tried to contact a friend of Pinky at an American air base which alerted the U.S. Air Force to or presence and luckily, they tracked our travels. The Russian group caught up with us on the way to the Catskills and a fighter jet took them out when they tried to kill us. If the U.S. Airforce had not intervened, we would have been wiped out by our chasers. That is when Sir George came into the picture. He soon realised what had happened and asked us to help in finding the group who had infiltrated the British Security services. What we didn't know is just had big the defections and infiltrations was. It was all through the services." "So that is how you joined Sir George?" "Yes, look, let's get some food and we will continue this over a coffee. "Good idea, where do you suggest?" "I don't often use this place but before you go home, you deserve a treat. Let's go to the Savoy." "Great it is on the service expenses." It was a bright day with the sun shining as they strolled up the Embankment. They didn't speak as they enjoyed the view. The Boats up and down the Thames, some with parties on board and other small crafts with all sorts of goods on them. They passed the Royal Albert Hall and headed for Charing Cross station and onto The Strand and the Savoy. Freddy knew the doorman, who was an ex. R.A.F. senior aircrafts man. He greeted Freddy and showed them in to the restaurant nodding to the restaurant reception as he led them straight to a table for two. "Damn nice chap that, he obviously knows you." "Yes, we trained together at Bridgenorth, basic training. He fell fowl of a Wolverhampton Wanderer and eventually they married but they separated some time ago, shame." They ordered a slap-up lunch and took a great deal of time in the lounge with a series of coffees. "Well, to continue. Sir George brought us back to Blighty and we started to investigate but we were still being followed as the Russians thought that we knew too much and we were chased all over by another extermination group." "You have just had a great time, haven't you." "Oh yes, everybody should have such fun. We started where we knew people from the kidnap and traced through them to people in high places. The poor chap who looked after us at the lock up was killed and his son took over. They were nice people and not involved at all. Anyway, we were chased all over by the Russian group and they lost out when they tried to kill us in a safe house. Sir George was waiting for them with armed agents. The infiltration was indeed very serious they had a spy in just about every area of our security system. We tried to capture someone who had knowledge of the Russian operation but they all eventually died in a shootout. Bellinger was our best bet when he tried to escape to the Russian side but near the Friedrich Strasse crossing, he tried to make a run for it and was taken out by the German police. If he hadn't shot at the German police he would have been taken into custody." "So, there is no one alive who was involved?" The only one that we could not expose as we hadn't enough evidence was the Home Secretary." "Wow it was as bad as that?" "I said that it was serious, yes, he was the leading light for the whole organisation and his deputy was Bellinger. The Home Secretary had to resign and his excuse for resigning was through bad health." "That doesn't seem to be of much help?" "Well, it's possible that there is still a loose end to catch up on but I don't see any at the moment." They finished the last of their coffee and set off back to the office. The sun shone and the day became warm and pleasant as they strolled back down the embankment. There was not a lot to discuss and they walked in silence, watching the river traffic again as they went. Freddy was trying not to look back over their conversation but he couldn't help it. Who was left to follow up on, he thought but nothing came to mind, except, the thought occurred that the only one of the Russian agents left alive was the past Home Secretary. Could he be involved? It seemed very unlikely seeing the type of persons involved. He did not appear to be inclined in that sexual direction but one never knows. "You said that you felt that you were being followed and there is a motorcyclist trailing slowly behind us." "I won't look and don't turn in their direction but where is it?" "One eighty degrees behind you." "Let us just pause to look at the river." They leaned on the wall and Freddy casually looked behind them. The Bike had stopped about a hundred yards away and the rider was covered in black leather and dark glass helmet. There was no way of identifying who it was. As they started on their way they strolled very slowly and the bike did not move. Tony looked round and the bike took off and it was obvious that they realised that they had been spotted. "Sorry about that, I couldn't resist a look as the bike that the rider was on is like the one that I have finished rebuilding. You know that I am a keen motorcyclist." "No problem, I was tempted to look as well. Was that the Bugatti?" "Yes, a very nice machine." "There is no way of knowing who that was but it is certainly a coincidence." "They have been following since e left our coffee house." "So, it wasn't by chance, they had to been aware where we were, which means that they followed us to lunch, interesting." "When we get back, I will make out my report on what I can make of it all and it might help you to get some idea of the challenges that you face." "Thanks Tony, that would be a great help. You are setting off home tonight?" "Yes, but if I come up with anything, I will let you know." They walked back to the office and kept an eye out for any followers but they were alone.

CHAPTER 28

Tony had left his report which confirmed the findings but had no leads to follow. The report had been left for Freddy two weeks before and there had been no incidents or signs of any followers. Freddy and Sir George were hoping that at last the affair could be closed. After going over all of the evidence, there was no trail to check up on. Freddy was stood down and he headed for home. He was not satisfied with the situation but there was no more that he could do. After Freddy had left, Sir George decided to step down and take retirement. He had been shocked and saddened by his arrest and accusations he no longer had faith in the system that he had supported for so long. He had sent a letter to Freddy to let him know of his decision and informed him of his successor. Freddy was not committed to take on the role of Huntley with the new head of Security but he had the option if he was needed. There would be a new team after his retirement which was at the end of the following month.

Freddy read the letter at home and was surprised, at first but then realised that Sir George had gone through a very trying time and he understood his reasoning. He considered his own future now. Freddy was independently financially secure and did not need to work or be employed in any way but he realised that as Huntley Haverstock he had been totally involved and distracted. What was he to do in the future? He was still not satisfied that it was all over, there were too many unanswered questions but without Sir George there was not a lot that he could do. He decided that he would take a break and not leave no information of where he was headed. A few days later, Freddy had packed and loaded his car for a tour around Europe. He suddenly realised that he had no friends to contact and no relationship with any member of the opposite sex. It was quite a bombshell and he became aware that his whole personal life had been on hold. He resolved to change that now. There was just one thing to complete and that was the death of the M.P. He travelled to Middlesbrough where his death had occurred and followed up the witnesses. He had the file with him and noted that a Carolyn had found the M.P. first. Freddy called at the address given as Carolyn's and was as surprised as she was when their eyes met. They had met briefly before Freddy joined the service and then lost touch when the Cuban affair blew up. They hadn't seen each other for many years. "Hello." Stuttered Freddy and the reply from Carolyn, just as tentative. "I was making enquiries about the M.P. that you found. May I come in?" "Of course." Freddy was shown into the lounge and was offered a cup of tea. "Yes, please." Carolyn went to put the kettle on. Freddy looked around the lounge and saw the photographs of Carloyn's family. It had been so long since their last meeting, Freddy could hardly remember the faces on the photographs. Carolyn brought a tray of tea, cups and cakes." I was just looking at the family photos and I can hardly recognise the family, it has been so long. What have you been up to? Are you still working at the Estate agents? How have you been all this time?" "You haven't changed you still want to know all the ins and outs of everything. Never mind about me, what have you been up to? I heard that you had something to do with the Government or Ministry?" "I have been working with Sir George Curswell at the Ministry on various projects but I may not be required any more so, I am taking some time for myself in Sicily." "Wow, I have always wanted to go somewhere like that. It sounds so romantic and different." "So, what have you been up to?" "Well, I lost the last of my family last year and I haven't worked since, everything was left to me by my parents and aunts and Uncles so I haven't needed to work. I have taken early retirement." "That's great, aren't you bored?" "Well, not really, I was just looking to book a holiday. The cost of them has gone through the roof. Have you been to Sicily before Freddy?" "Yes, I have friends there and I going to travel there as soon as I complete my business here. I hope that you won't be offended but a thought occurred to me, would you like to come and stay with my friends in Sicily. I hope that I am not being too forward?" "Not at all, what a good idea and I am sure that it will not be as expensive as a tour holiday." "Great, I will let them know that you will be joining me. I don't know how long I will be staying there. Does that make any difference?" "No, I have nothing else planned and if I like it I might stay on a while." "That's settled then." They had finished their tea and cakes. "I just need to know if you knew anything about the M.P. that you found." "All that I know is that I nearly fell over his body and the neighbour called the police. I was questioned by the police as if I had been involved but all I did was stumble on him. I know nothing other than that." "Thanks Carolyn. Look, I will give you telephone number and if you need to call me for any reason I will get back to you tomorrow anyway and I will book our flights for the day after tomorrow. Is that okay? What's your number?" They exchanged telephone numbers and Freddy left for the local police. After visiting the police station, it was clear that no one knew any more about events and it proved to be a blank end. It would just have to be written off in his final report. The next day he completed his report and sent it to Sir George's office with a update of his travelling plans but without any mention of Carolyn. He wasn't going to have the office staff smirking up their sleeves. He contacted Carolyn later that day and told her of the flight details and timings and he planned to pick her up in good time. Carolyn was quite excited by the news. Freddy could not get away from the feeling that the events of the past with this case were not right. He had drawn a blank with the M.P. He knew who was responsible but why? It made no real sense that Sir George was such a target and he had been included as a target as his assistant. He decided that he was ready to have a break and come back to it sometime later. He packed for Sicily and picked up Carolyn and headed for the airport. As he left his house he glanced behind him and saw a girl on a bicycle, he had seen that girl before but he was on a mission and drove off at speed to catch the plane for Sicily.

They arrived at Comiso airport and true to form, they were met by Ricardo. It was an emotional meeting and Ricardo was so pleased to see Carolyn with Freddy, he had them married already as soon as he saw them. Both Freddy and Carolyn were a bit embarrassed but smiled at the assumption. They looked at each other and coloured up. Ricardo took them to his house in Ragusa and were welcomed like long lost family by all. Francesca Millotti was extra excited to see Freddy again, she had lots of news for him about her meeting with a new man in her life, she couldn't wait to tell Freddy. Ricardo ordered coffee and Amaretti biscuits and they went onto the terrace. "Francesca has been bursting to tell you about the new man in her life, it looks as if she has found the right one this time, nothing like the one that you disposed of. Tell Freddy about your man Francesca." "He proposed to me last night." "You did not tell me." Said Ricardo. "Yes, I accepted of course. His name is Custanzu and he will be here this afternoon to speak to Ricardo. I am sorry that I did not tell you but it wasn't certain that he was coming today as he hadn't told his family until this morning. His father was delighted and will be arranging to meet up with Ricardo later this week." "You have dropped your father into it, haven't you." "You are not wrong Freddy, who would have daughters? Now she tells me. There will be much business to discuss when two families are joined by a marriage." Freddy thought that there certainly would be some problems to sort out as the two families just about controlled the whole of Sicily, though neither family would admit to it. Ricardo left with apologies to make his preparations for the family meetings. "I think that you have just ruffled Ricardo's feathers with your news, Francesca." "Yes, I am sorry that things were not as we had hoped for our announcement. You will like Custanzu, he is very cuddly and nice." "I am sure that I will, if you say so." Carolyn had been quiet for a long time listening, "Will Ricardo be upset now?" "He may be but he will soon be happy for me. Custanzu and I will be going on a trip together when everything is agreed by the families and I will ask them to have you and Carolyn as our chapperones, will you do that for us?" "Of course I will, how about you Carolyn?" "I would be honoured." "That is settled then. I will make all the arrangements and we will have a great time together and maybe there will be two marriages?" Freddy and Carolyn exchanged glances. Later that day Custanzu called on Richardo to ask for Francesca's hand in marriage. He was built like a front row forward and could easily be a player for Italy in the rugby union six nations, he must have weighed twenty-four stones. All must have gone well as he joined Francesca and they were both smiling. "We will be leaving tomorrow for the feast of Saint Agatha in Catania. Custanzu has family there and they haven't heard the news yet so we will combine the two things in one. Your aunty will be over the moon with our news she has been going on about us getting together for months now." "Yes, she is a proper fuss pot but she will have to make a fuss somehow." "I hope that you are both okay with that?" "Of course, we look forward to joining in the feast celebrations. I have heard so much about them and we do not want any earthquakes from Mount Etna." "Ah, you Know about

Saint Agatha?" "I have been told by Ricardo that it is a great celebration." "Yes, the festival of Saint Agatha takes place in Catania in the first week of February Sicilians celebrate Saint Agatha for her purported intercession to avert danger during eruptions of Mount Etna, earthquakes, and some epidemics that had affected Catania. The three-day festival begins at noon on February 3 with a procession known as "della luminaria". *Cannalori*, eleven large candles in baroque gilt casings that proceeds from the [Church of Sant'Agata alla Fornace](#) to the [Cathedral of St. Agatha](#). Each *candelora* represents one of the medieval guilds. At 3.00 PM, a cross-country race takes place through the streets of town. This is followed in the evening by a concert in the [Piazza del Duomo](#) and fireworks. The next day, after the "Messa dell'Aurora", mass at dawn, a reliquary-bust of St. Agatha atop a silver *fercola* or carriage leaves the cathedral and is pulled through the neighbourhoods, passing places associated with the life of the saint. The devoted followers wear the traditional white tunic that covers the body down to the ankles and is tied at the waist with a rope. The celebrations continue through the night. Gaily decorated kiosks sell traditional street food such as *arancini* (rice balls) and beccafico sardines (with breadcrumbs, pine nuts and raisins). On the 5th, there is again a procession after Mass. The heavy silver carriage is pulled up a steep slope. Successful passage is considered to bode well for the rest of the year." "Wow, that is some celebration and it the first of February today." "Yes, we will get there in time for the start." "It sounds as if we are in for a treat, thank you for inviting us. What do you think Carolyn?" "I agree, it sounds wonderful." "That is settled then, we leave in the morning. I will go and tell Ricardo of our plans." Francesca left the room with a skip and a big smile on her face. She looked very happy as she left and Custanzu also glowed with pride as he watched her go.

Custanzo arrived the next morning in a large black limo. And all the bags were loaded into a spacious boot. As they climbed aboard, Freddy could not help think that the car was typical of the Mafia's image and he was now a part of it. Francesca told them of the arrangements and all was paid for in advance by their parents, everything was booked first class. Custanzo's parents had also provided a driver so that both couples could be together for the duration. Freddy looked at Carolyn and thought that maybe, if she was of the same feeling, there could be a joint wedding. He had been so glad to have met up with her again, if things originally had gone to plan, they might already have been married. That was put to the test when they got to the hotel in Catania, double rooms had been booked for each couple. Someone was determined to get them together and Freddy did not think that it was Ricardo. Carolyn stood in their room and looked at Freddy, "What are we going to do?" "It was booked deliberately by someone to get us together. If you are okay to go along with them, so am I. I was really sorry that we were parted so long ago and I am really pleased to be back with you." Carolyn moved towards Freddy and gave him a big hug. "If you are happy with the room, then, so am I." Freddy could not believe that she felt the same and he gave her a long and lingering kiss. "Shall we get married Carolyn?" Carolyn smiled and then spoke, "Yes."

When the news came out Francesca informed the families and plans were put in place for an immediate church ceremony for both couples. Francesca was overjoyed. The families arranged to join them in Catania after the festival finished which left them a few days together.

The festival went as expected and they all had a great time. The parades were spectacular and the entertainment was non-stop. Cuatanzo's aunt had been to the church and made all plans to give the couples a wedding to remember and the local hotel was completely booked for the reception. Freddy could not believe what had been put in place and he and Carolyn were feeling very honoured to be a part of it all. The families were due to arrive the next morning after the festival and their final night before the invasion Freddy and Carolyn consummated their relationship in glorious sex. This had not been their first time but it was so romantic and meaningful for both of them. Carolyn was a bit concerned that, this time, it had been too successful. Is wasn't long before she found that she was with child.

When they returned to Ricardo's there was a message waiting for him. Sir George had been attacked again but the assailant had missed the target and had left him with a bullet in his leg. Freddy had been asked to return to London and assist in the investigation, he was Huntley again. Both he and Carolyn were disappointed with the news that they would have to cut short their honeymoon but they both accepted the situation and promised themselves that soon they would continue their celebration. They had their tickets booked for London by Ricardo, who was sorry that they had to leave so early. They promised to return at the first possible opportunity. The flight was straight forward and Freddy dropped Carolyn at his London apartment before turning up at Sir George's office.

CHAPTER 29

Sir George was bandaged up to his knee and he was pleased to see Huntley again. "We thought that we had completed the investigation but there is obviously someone left who holds a grudge. I hear that you have been married during your leave?" "I was stood down, Sir, not on leave. Yes, I met the girl that I had. intended to marry years ago. We met up again and we were railroaded into making it official by some enthusiastic Sicilians." "Well, you are needed again, as you know more about this case than anyone else." "Did you have any idea who did this to you?" "No but there was a girl on a bicycle who was a witness. I was just coming to the office but at the entrance I felt a severe pain in my leg, apparently this girl was cycling past but did not see who fired at me." "That is a coincidence, I have seen a girl on a cycle a couple of times. I don't like coincidences. Can you describe her?" "Late twenties or early thirties, red cycle helmet and blue coat. That's all I can remember but she was interviewed by the police and they have her details, I think." "Great, who was the officer in charge?" "I don't know the chap but he is a new chief at the Met. Called Forrest." "Thank you, Sir, I will get onto it immediately." Huntley left the office and headed straight for the Met. Headquarters. He had a word with Chief Inspector Forrest and he was given the information on the girl on the cycle. He headed straight for the address given only to find that it was a false address. It was now becoming clear that this girl was not just a passer-by, she could be the assailant or clearly involved. He had been given a photograph of the girl and he had the help of some officers allocated to him to make enquiries. Each had been given a copy of the photo. It wasn't long before the girl was known. A neighbour identified the girl as Gail Pickhill and she lived opposite her in a rented house. She wasn't there all the time but she was a regular and she had had a lot of visitors over the time that she had rented. Huntley went to records to see what they had on Miss Pickhill. As he waited for the record office to get back to him, he realised that the name was familiar. Pickhill was the Russian group leader and Home Secretary at the time of his first encounter with Sir George. He immediately asked records for any connection. It soon came back the Home Secretary at that time had a daughter call Gail. He set up all points search for the missing girl.

Back at the office Sir George and Huntley discussed the results and concluded that they might have the answer to all the troubles of the recent past. Gail Pickhill was taken into custody and transported to the ministry offices. Sir George and Huntley interviewed her.

"Your father was the Home Secretary?" There was no reply. "We know that You are the daughter of the Home Secretary, so why are you not answering?" There was a snarl and outburst from Gail. "You are the bastard who drove my father to his death. I swore at his bedside before he died that I would get revenge after what you did to him. He was a good man and in high office and you took it away from him." She had to be restrained by the police woman stood with her. "You made him resign for no good reason and he was so hurt that he gave up on life and you are responsible for his death. I was helped by the team of my father but you killed all of them so I had to do it myself. I wish that I hadn't missed you outside your office. You are just as responsible Haverstock and you were lucky to have survived." She flopped down into her chair. Sir George and Huntley looked at each other and Huntley addressed the girl. "You had no idea that your father was a Russian agent. You had no knowledge that he had no choice but to resign?"

"Liar." She glared at them and they looked back at her. She had no idea of the truth about her own father. "Liar, liar, lies." She screamed. It was silent for what seemed ages before she burst into tears. Sir George had brought the report on her father's case and put the papers in front of her. She stared at them and slowly read the report. Huntley and Sir George took their leave and headed back to the office. Sir George had difficulty walking but with a little assistance he made it. "Well, that takes the biscuit, Gail had been the cause of all of those deaths and for what?" Huntley replied "Ignorance. She was totally in the dark about her father's activities and employed a bunch of killers to do her dirty work." "I really do think that, this time, it has reached a conclusion Sir." "I believe that you are right. I am stepping down now as head of security, I have had enough. It is time for me to take it easy for a change. I have set everything in motion for my retirement and my replacement." "That means that I will be stepped down as Huntley?" "Yes, all will come out tomorrow as I have arranged for a departmental announcement in the meeting room at ten o'clock. I will see you there." It was a long night but it was pleasant to have Carolyn with him.

The next day at the meeting the department had the whole affair laid out for them. There were a few gasps as the tale was told. Sir George told them of his plan to retire and with immediate effect. What had been agreed was Sir George's replacement and the job was offered to Freddy Goodchild. Freddy was taken aback. "I will have to think about this. I have just married and we have not had our honeymoon so I ask that I have some time to consider." The meeting agreed to defer appointment until after Freddy's honeymoon.

Carolyn was thrilled by the news and happy that Freddy had time to make up his mind. They decided to return to Sicily and meet up with Francesca and Custanzu again. Ricardo was there to meet them again.

All characters in this story are total fiction and refer to no persons, living or dead.

www.ingramcontent.com/pod-product-compliance
Lightning Source LLC
Chambersburg PA
CBHW061229070526
44584CB00030B/4054